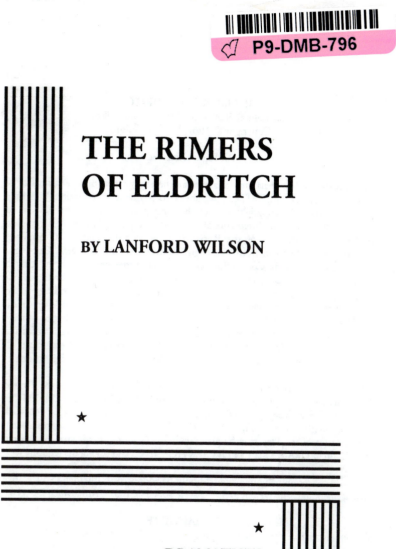

THE RIMERS
OF ELDRITCH

BY LANFORD WILSON

DRAMATISTS
PLAY SERVICE
INC.

SPECIAL NOTE

THE RIMERS OF ELDRITCH was first presented by Theatre 1967 (Richard Barr, Clinton Wilder, Edward Albee) at the Cherry Lane Theatre, in New York City, on February 20, 1967. The production was a project of Albarwild Theater Arts Inc. It was directed by Michael Kahn, and designed by William Ritman. The cast, in order of speaking, was as follows:

WILMA ATKINS	Dena Dietrich
MARTHA TRUIT	Kate Wilkinson
NELLY WINDROD	Blanche Dee
JUDGE—PREACHER	James Noble
MARY WINDROD	Bette Henritze
ROBERT CONKLIN	Don Scardino
A TRUCKER	Richard Orzel
CORA GROVES	Ruth Manning
WALTER	Kevin O'Connor
EVA JACKSON	Amy Taubin
JOSH JOHNSON	Walter Hadler
SKELLY MANNOR	John O'Leary
PECK JOHNSON	Alfred Hinckley
MAVIS JOHNSON	Helen Stenborg
PATSY JOHNSON	Susan Tyrrell
EVELYN JACKSON	Elizabeth Moore
LENA TRUIT	Katherine Bruce

The publisher gratefully acknowledges the assistance of Mr. Donald Koehler, stage manager of the above production, in preparing the play for publication.

TIME

The Present. The play covers a period during the Spring, Summer and Fall of the year.

LOCATION

Eldritch, a small former mining town in the Middle West; population about seventy.

CHARACTERS

ROBERT CONKLIN, a boy eighteen, small, quiet.

EVA JACKSON, a crippled girl fourteen.

EVELYN JACKSON, her mother.

NELLY WINDROD, a strong woman middle-aged.

MARY WINDROD, her retarded, aged mother.

PATSY JOHNSON, a pretty high school student.

MAVIS JOHNSON, her mother.

PECK JOHNSON, her father.

JOSH JOHNSON, her brother.

LENA TRUIT, her girlfriend the same age.

MARTHA TRUIT, Lena's mother.

WILMA ATKINS, a friend of Lena's mother.

SKELLY MANNOR, the town hermit-shutout, about sixty.

PREACHER ⎫
⎬ played by the same actor, mid-fifties.
JUDGE ⎭

CORA GROVES, the owner of Hilltop Cafe.

WALTER, her young lover.

A TRUCKER who stops by the cafe.

The action of the play takes place during the Spring, Summer and Fall. Time should be suggested by shifting of lights, grouping of characters. The set is a series of areas, perhaps levels with porch and courtroom railings. Most all the characters of the play are on stage throughout the two acts, grouping as needed to suggest time and place.

6

The Rimers of Eldritch

ACT I

Lights are preset to dimly light stage with platforms taking on a glow. When house lights out actors enter from R. and L. When actors in position lights dim out and area light comes up on Judge in C. of top platform followed by light on Martha and Wilma sitting D. L. Wilma and Martha are seated suggesting an evening, in the Spring, rocking on the porch.

JUDGE. Nelly Windrod, do you solemnly swear to tell the truth and nothing but the truth so help you God?

WILMA. (*Seated on a porch with Martha.*) Well, what I heard isn't fit for talk, but I heard that Mrs. Cora Groves, up on the highway?

MARTHA. Yes.

WILMA. Has taken a boy, she's old enough to be his mother on, and is keeping him up there in her cafe.

MARTHA. In her bed.

WILMA. (*With true sympathy.*) That woman went crazy when her husband left her.

MARTHA. Oh, I know she did.

WILMA. That woman, I swear, isn't responsible for her own actions. (*A very faint light begins to illuminate the "court room," Nelly standing, her hand raised.*)

MARTHA. I should say she isn't.

WILMA. I hear he does things around the cafe, whistling around like he belonged there.

MARTHA. Have you ever heard anything like it?

WILMA. I haven't, I swear to God. (*Lights go up on Nelly. Nelly is standing in "jury box" which is second platform R. C.*)

NELLY. I do. (*Lights out on Nelly.*)

MARTHA. Why, she called Evelyn Jackson a liar to her face,

and Eva too. Swore things the devil and his angels wouldn't believe it. She'd stand up there and swear black was white.

WILMA. And Nelly, poor woman, the life that woman leads. Only God in His Heaven knows the trials that woman has to bear.

MARTHA. That she should have to be dragged through this.

WILMA. She stood there and told the way it was; I said to Mrs. Jackson—

MARTHA. —I know—

WILMA. Cried the whole time—

MARTHA. I saw.

WILMA. —Only God in Heaven knows the trials that poor woman has had to bear. (*Lights fill stage and all actors in "court" stand. Light focuses on Nelly. Martha rises.*)

JUDGE. Nelly Windrod, do you solemnly swear to tell the whole truth, and nothing but the truth—

NELLY. (*Quietly troubled.*) I do, yes.

JUDGE. —so help you God?

NELLY. I do. (*Lights like a blink of the eye—lights down and up on Nelly.*)

JUDGE. (*Exactly as before.*) Nelly Windrod, do you solemnly swear to tell the whole truth, and nothing but the truth, so help you God?

NELLY. I do. Yes. (*Lights fade out on all. The* D. L. *light on Martha and Wilma up.*)

MARTHA. (*Standing.*) So help me God I don't know how we let him hang around here like he did. Not talking to nobody.

WILMA. Nobody I know of could live like that.

MARTHA. Like that time he scared young Patsy so bad.

WILMA. Bad for the whole town with someone like that.

MARTHA. Like that way he had of just standing around.

WILMA. Around here everybody knows everybody.

MARTHA. Everybody was scared of him. Everybody knew what he was.

WILMA. A fool like that.

MARTHA. Grumbling and mumbling around; standing and watching it all.

WILMA. I'd think people'd feel easier now. I know I swear I do. (*Lights go out. Lights come up on "court" and all focus on Nelly.*)

MARTHA. I do.

8

NELLY. I do. (*Beat.*)

JUDGE. (*Lights fade out on "court" and Robert crosses* C. *to Mary.*) Now, Miss Windrod, if you would tell the court, in your own words . . . (*Lights up* D. C. *area, for Robert and Mary. Martha sits.*)

MARY. (*To Robert.*) Now, we have to understand that Nelly is my flesh and blood.

ROBERT. I know.

MARY. Yes, love, she's my flesh and blood and she thinks she knows but she doesn't know but she thinks she does.

ROBERT. I suppose she does if anybody does.

MARY. Well, she thinks she does. But I know and you know. I was at my window, watching the moon.

ROBERT. Was there a moon?

MARY. You know there was. I'll tell it the way it was. I said to those people, all those new people in town—there isn't much to know about Eldritch, used to be Elvin Eldritch's pasture till it gave out I guess and they found coal. It was built on coal. Built on coal with coal money and deserted when the coal gave out and here it stands, this wicked old town. All the buildings bowing and nodding.

ROBERT. How do you know so much?

MARY. And still so little? I would puzzle that if I could. I told them none of the people here now were coal people; they are store owners and farmers and the mining people moved off. They raped the land and moved away; there used to be explosives that rattled the windows, oh my, and shook the water in a bucket, day and night.

ROBERT. How come you remember so much?

MARY. And still so little? The last time I saw you, why, you was just a little baby; you've grown up so.

ROBERT. You saw me yesterday, Mrs. Windrod.

MARY. You don't know. Isn't that sweet. The last I saw you, why, you weren't no bigger than that high.

ROBERT. You've known me all my . . .

MARY. (*Robert crosses to* R. *of second platform.*) You've grown up so. I have terrible bruises on my arm there. Look at that. (*Light fades out on Mary* C. *and comes up on Cora's "cafe"* D. R. *and Wilma and Martha* D. L.)

9

TRUCKER. (*Leaving the counter of Cora's cafe. Walter is seated at the "counter."*) I'll see you, Cora.

CORA. Can't avoid it, I guess. You watch it now on those narrow roads.

TRUCKER. It's push-pull with the load; I'll come back through empty day after tomorrow, you remember to tell me that again.

CORA. Stay awake now.

TRUCKER. (*Crosses* U. R. *to Johnson family.*) No danger of that.

WILMA. I'll say one thing for her. How long has it been he's been there?

CORA. (*To Walter.*) Boy.

MARTHA. Two or three months now nearly. Walks around the place whistling like he owned it.

WILMA. Well, he earns his keep.

CORA. Boy.

MARTHA. It's not in the kitchen that he earns his keep, Wilma.

CORA. Boy.

WILMA. Well, I'll say one thing—

CORA. —I'm getting ready to close up now.

WILMA. —Whatever it is she looks a darn sight better now than she did a year ago. Since I can remember.

CORA. Boy.

WALTER. (*As though waking from a daydream.*) I'm sorry.

CORA. I'm fixing to close up. You sleeping?

WALTER. Thinking, I guess.

CORA. Have another cup of coffee, I got time.

MARTHA. That woman isn't responsible for her own actions since her husband left her.

WALTER. Swell.

WILMA. It's not for us to judge.

MARTHA. That's all well and good but anyone who deliberately cuts herself off from everybody else in town.

WILMA. I don't judge, but I know who I speak to on the street and who I don't.

WALTER. Is there work here in town do you know?

CORA. Down in Eldritch? Not if you're looking for wages. Not here.

MARTHA. It's easy to see the devil's work.

WALTER. I had that in mind.

10

CORA. You might try Centerville; Eldritch is all but a ghost town.

WALTER. You here alone?

CORA. I've managed for seven years; it hasn't bothered me.

WALTER. It might not be a bad idea to take someone on yourself.

WILMA. It's a sin to sashay through Centerville the way she does, buying that boy shirts and new clothes. Keeping him up on the highway.

MARTHA. I don't go, but I understand he's made a showplace out of her cafe.

WILMA. I'd be happier if it was me if they made her close it down.

MARTHA. It ought to be against the law serving beer to truck drivers and them having to be on the road so much.

WILMA. The wages of sin lead to death.

CORA. Aren't you cold in just that jacket; that's pretty light for April.

WALTER. No, it's not bad. (*They regard each other a moment, lights fade out on "cafe" and up on Mary* c. *Lights remain on Martha and Wilma.*)

MARTHA. The wages of sin lead to death.

WILMA. Bless her heart, poor old thing.

MARTHA. (*As Mary Windrod passes the "porch."*) Good evening, Mary.

WILMA. Good evening, Mary Windrod.

MARY. (*She stops.*) You two. I watch you two sometimes. (*Mary talks, almost with everything she says, as though she were describing a beautiful dream to a pet canary.*)

WILMA. Aren't you cold in that shawl, dear?

MARTHA. Nights are cold in this valley for June.

MARY. It's not bad.

WILMA. You'll be catching a chill next.

MARY. I was once a nurse and I believe that the constant proximity to sickness has given me an immunity to night air.

MARTHA. Never think that.

MARY. Us dry old women rattle like paper; we couldn't get sick. I listen to you old women sometimes.

WILMA. How's your daughter?

MARY. Yes, indeed.

MARTHA. I beg your pardon?

11

MARY. The proximity to all that sickness.

WILMA. Yes, love.

MARY. Immunity to death itself. My number passed Gabriel right on by. It came up and passed right on by and here I am a forgotten child.

WILMA. You better get inside, love. (*Martha rises.*)

MARY. Rusting away, flaking away. (*Mary crosses up on step to second platform.*)

MARTHA. You get in, now.

MARY. This wicked town. God hear a dried up woman's prayer and do not forgive this wicked town! (*Lights come up on congregation. The congregation bursts into "Shall We Gather At The River"; only a few bars, the song fades. [Note: Words of hymn given at back of book.] The congregation disperses. Lights brighten and focus on "court." All focus on Nelly.*)

NELLY. (*Over the last of the song.*) And mama came running downstairs and said a man had attacked young Eva Jackson.

JUDGE. Would you point out Eva . . .

NELLY. There, poor lamb, can't hardly speak two words since this thing happened and I don't wonder— (*Lights fade out on "court" and focus on Martha and Wilma. Martha sits.*)

WILMA. (*As Nelly fades, over a word or two.*) Well, I know I swear I don't know what he sees in her. (*Eva crosses from U. L.— to second platform to C. as lights come up.*)

MARTHA. It's nice of him though.

WILMA. Well, I know but Driver Junior's old enough to be taking girls out; he shouldn't be wandering around with her. (*Robert begins to cross D. C. from R. of second platform.*)

MARTHA. It's nice to have somebody to keep her company. Still and all it doesn't seem natural, I know what you mean.

WILMA. I don't know what he sees in her. (*Lights fade out on Martha and Wilma.*)

MARTHA. Poor thing.

ROBERT. Eva!

EVA. Are you glad to be out of school?

ROBERT. I liked it all right.

EVA. What are you going to be?

ROBERT. Who knows?

EVA. I bet I know what you won't be, don't I?

12

ROBERT. What's that?

EVA. A race car driver.

ROBERT. Why do you want to say that? You think I couldn't do that if I wanted to?

EVA. You don't want to get yourself killed.

ROBERT. Driver didn't want it, he just had an accident.

EVA. You want to be like him?

ROBERT. People don't want to do the same thing their brother did; I couldn't see any sense in it.

EVA. I knew you didn't. You aren't going to get yourself killed.

ROBERT. Killed doesn't have anything to do with it. Eva, good Lord, I don't want people carrying on like that; honking their horns, coming into town every week like a parade. I never even went to see Driver.

EVA. You decided what you want to be?

ROBERT. I don't have to decide this minute, do I?

EVA. I just wondered.

ROBERT. Do you know? You don't know what you want.

EVA. Of course I know; you know, I told you. So do you know, everybody knows what they want it's what they think they really can do that they don't know.

ROBERT. Well, I don't have to decide yet.

EVA. When's it gonna be autumn? I love autumn so much I could hug it. I want it to be autumn. That's what I want right now. Now. Autumn. Now. (*This last as though conjuring.*)

ROBERT. Good luck; I don't see it.

EVA. (*In a burst.*) Don't you be derisive to me, Driver Junior!

ROBERT. Don't call me that.

EVA. Well, don't you go on Robert Conklin or I'll call you anything I like.

ROBERT. You'll be talking to yourself.

EVA. Everybody else calls you that. Don't go away; I won't, I promise. Don't you wish it was autumn? Don't you? Don't you love autumn? And the wind and rime and pumpkins and gourds and corn shocks? I won't again. Don't you love autumn? Don't you Robert? I won't call you that. Everybody else does but I won't.

ROBERT. I haven't thought about it.

EVA. Well, think about it, right now. Think about how it smells.

ROBERT. How does it smell?

EVA. Like dry, windy, cold, frosty rime and chaff and leaf smoke and corn husks.

ROBERT. It does, huh?

EVA. Pretend. Close your eyes. Are your eyes closed? Don't you wish it was here? Like apples and cider. You go.

ROBERT. And rain.

EVA. Sometimes. And potatoes and flower seeds and honey.

ROBERT. And popcorn and butter.

EVA. (*Opening her eyes.*) Yes. Oh, it does not! You're not playing at all. There's hay and clover and alfalfa and all that. (*Hitting him, really quite hard, slapping.*)

ROBERT. (*Laughing.*) Come on, it's different for everybody.

EVA. Well, that's not right; it doesn't at all. Are you making fun?

ROBERT. Come on, don't be rough.

EVA. I will too; you're not the least bit funny, Driver Junior! (*As he starts to walk to second platform.*) Come back here, Robert! Robert Conklin. Driver Junior! Little brother. You brother was a man, anyway. Coward. Robert? Bobby? (*Robert crosses to* L. *Lights fade on Eva as she moves* D. R. C. *and Wilma crosses to second platform, which is now the "store."*)

WILMA. And I'll have some flour and yeast. And three packs of sure-jell.

ROBERT. Right you are; how much flour?

WILMA. No more than five pounds in this weather. How are you doin'·in school?

ROBERT. All right.

WILMA. I just said to Martha Truit, I suppose Driver Junior will be leaving us as soon as school gets out next month. Leaving us pretty soon, anyway, like all the young kids now.

ROBERT. Not for a while yet.

WILMA. Oh, you will; you'll be going off to see the world.

ROBERT. I don't know.

WILMA. There's nothing for a strong young man in this dead old town. Where do you think you'll be heading?

ROBERT. I don't know.

WILMA. Des Moines?

ROBERT. I don't imagine.

WILMA. St. Louis?

ROBERT. Who knows?

14

WILMA. Chicago?

ROBERT. I might not leave at all for a while.

WILMA. Well, your brother stayed and he was wonderful but we all expect you to be moving along like all the young boys now.

ROBERT. I don't know. (*Wilma crosses to sit by Martha. Lights fade out on store and come up on top platform where Nelly has hold of Mary as if shaking truth from her. Nelly has a hold on her arm. She is turning backward, Nelly forward, avoiding the raised hand threatening her. Much as on a turntable going backwards.*)

MARY. I know, I know, I know, I know, don't hit me; don't hit me, baby.

NELLY. What do you mean telling people a tale like that. You know I bought that mill.

MARY. You bought it, baby; I know you bought it. (*Skelly crosses to post D. R.*)

NELLY. Well, they said in town you told I'd killed dad to get it.

MARY. I said he died mysteriously.

NELLY. He died of old age, he was ninety-six for God's sakes.

MARY. He died mysteriously!

NELLY. In his sleep like you will; died of old age like you will. What in hell do you mean telling something like that?

MARY. I didn't mean to, baby. I don't mean to—

NELLY. —You're batty as a goddamned loon.

MARY. They don't like me is what it is. They know I watch them. They don't like me in town, I knew they didn't. I don't say those things. They tell things on me.

NELLY. You're crazy as hell is what it is; you're out of your goddamned mind is what it is.

MARY. Baby, don't talk like that. They tell *fibs* on me. They say—

NELLY. Showing them bruises and saying I beat you; when the hell did I ever beat you? You know goddamned well how you get those bruises. You fall down! You bruise! You run into things! You're old. You bump things. Who the hell takes care of you and you telling lies on me like that, mama, what do you mean?

MARY. I don't mean to.

NELLY. They don't listen to you; to say things like that.

MARY. They don't listen to me, Nelly.

15

NELLY. It doesn't do you any good, they come right in and tell me.

MARY. Don't hurt me.

NELLY. I think you better go on up to your room! (*Starts to cross* R.)

MARY. No, don't lock the door.

NELLY. If I leave the house I'll lock the door or you'll wander out and get hurt. You'll fall down the stairs and tell I beat you.

MARY. I don't want to go up there; the evil town is all around me up there.

NELLY. Go upstairs mama.

MARY. It's painted on the windows—

NELLY. Well, pull the shades down if you don't want to see them. (*She sits on* D. R. *corner top platform.*)

MARY. My skin, whole body is just flaking away—this evil town! This evil town! (*Crosses* U. C. *to edge of top platform. Lights fade on top platform and come up dimly on Skelly as boys "Baa" from* U. R. *steps.*)

JOSH AND SEVERAL BOYS. (*Taunting Skelly, jeeringly.*) Baaa-aaaaaaaa! Baaaaaaaaaa! Baaaaaaaaa! Baaaaaaaa!

SKELLY. (*In a deep, mangled, growling almost drunken voice.*) Get on you son of bitch. Son of bitches. (*Sounding about like "Geah-own-ya-sansobith! Sansobith!"*)

THE BOYS. Baaaaaa! Baaaaaa!

SKELLY. Get the hell on you, get on! (*In a deep almost terrified growl.*) Go, go on, sonabith! (*Crosses* R. *of second platform.*)

NELLY. (*Steps into Skelly's light which is "jury box." Lights fade on Nelly and slowly move from "jury box" to top platform, to Cora's "cafe."*) And I heard something outside—

JUDGE. (*As the town becomes alive everywhere.*) A travesty of justice.

PECK. We of the jury—

CORA. Walter? (*The lights are moving like three hot spots without order from top platform to Cora's "cafe" to "jury box." Everything is sort of murky and the townspeople more like an improvisation from place to place.*)

PECK. Find Nelly Windrod—

CORA. Walter?

PECK. Not guilty.

MARTHA. Not guilty.
CORA. Walter?
EVA. Robert?
NELLY. Oh, god; mama?
EVELYN. Eva? (*The cord that holds the scene together is Evelyn calling from* U. L. *to Eva* D. R. *like from house to yard.*)
TRUCKER. Not guilty.
WILMA. Papa?
MAVIS. Peck?
JOSH. Not guilty.
WALTER. Cora!
CORA. Walter?
JUDGE. Not guilty.
PATSY. (*To Lena.*) I know.
EVELYN. Eva? You come on, now.
CORA. Oh, god, oh, god, oh, god, oh, god, oh, god.
JOSH. (*Has been whistling distantly for a dog. Calling softly.*) Blackie? Here, Blackie?
EVELYN. You better get on in here now.
EVA. I'm coming.
JOSH. (*Now Evelyn crosses to second platform* C. *and begins to open "door" to look for Eva.*) Come on, boy.
LENA. The poor thing.
PATSY. Really, I get so damn tired of all that nonsense.
LENA. I know, but they insist I wear it. (*Lights stop moving and lights up on* D. C. *area on Eva and Evelyn.*)
EVELYN. You better put a sweater on if you're going to sit out there. (*Crosses* D. *step.*)
EVA. (*Approaching the house.*) I'm coming in directly.
EVELYN. Not directly, you come on in now.
EVA. All right.
EVELYN. Where were you all day?
EVA. I was wandering around the woods.
EVELYN. Now, you know I don't want you running around alone. What if you fell and hurt yourself and who'd ever know it?
EVA. I wasn't alone; Robert and I went walking.
EVELYN. Well, don't you go off alone.
EVA. I won't.

EVELYN. Not all afternoon. Wandering around; God knows what could happen to you.

EVA. I know, I don't.

EVELYN. You look so fatigued.

EVA. I'm not at all.

EVELYN. I don't want you spending so much time with that boy.

EVA. What boy?

EVELYN. That Driver Junior. Wandering around with that boy. Spending all afternoon and evening with him.

EVA. Well who else would I spend it with?

EVELYN. Well, why do you have to go off every day of the week? Doing God knows what? You could visit the Stutses, you shouldn't be running around. It isn't good for you; you have to be careful. You're not like other kids; you know how easily you get fatigued; you run yourself out every day; perspiring like you do; wandering off with that boy. If something happened who'd know? And don't think he's responsible; his brother might have been different; devil and his angels wouldn't know if something happened. I don't know why you can't stay at home like everyone else. Traipsing around the woods half-naked, what do you do out there in the woods alone the two of you, anyhow?

EVA. Nothing.

EVELYN. I said you answer me.

EVA. (*Rapidly.*) Nothing!

EVELYN. I said you answer me the truth, young miss.

EVA. We don't do anything. Whatever you think.

EVELYN. Don't you talk back to me, what do you do little miss smarty pants? All day gone from the house, smarty? (*Hits her.*)

EVA. We talk.

EVELYN. You talk, you talk, I'll just bet you talk; now you get in that house this minute do you hear me!

EVA. (*Leaving.*) I don't know what you think. (*Crosses up steps c. to second platform and ends up in "witness box."*)

EVELYN. (*Crosses u. l. top platform.*) You get on in to the supper table! You're going to be the death of me. I swear, I swear, I swear. (*Lights change scene to the "court room."*)

JUDGE. —To tell the whole truth and nothing but the truth so help you God?

ROBERT. She didn't see anything.

18

JUDGE. Eva, as a witness to this terrible—

EVA. I don't know! I didn't see! I didn't see! I told you I didn't see anything! (*A long run into her mother's arms.*)

EVELYN. Leave my daughter alone! (*Cora crosses into "witness box" from* D. R.) Can't you see she's upset? My God, what are you trying to do to her?

CORA. (*Over same.*) She told me.

EVELYN. (*Crosses* L. C. *top platform.*) You know what I think of you? Before God!

CORA. She told me.

ROBERT. She didn't see.

EVA. I don't know!

NELLY. It's not true; none of it; it's like I said. You're trying to make me out a murderer; (*Lines overlap and "court" focuses on Judge* U. C.) it was god will be done.

CORA. She told me!

JUDGE. (*Over, rising above.*) We all have long known Skelly Mannor; we have known of his past—that latent evil in him; that unnatural desire and we have long been aware that at any time the bitterness in his soul might again overflow. (*General crowd murmur.*) We let things lie. We took no action to prevent his crime, the pending, at any moment crime; and the burden must be ours. We are all responsible for the shock to these two innocents. (*General murmur, several Amens.*) We are responsible for our actions; for allowing the heathen in our fold. (*The Judge's oratory slides into the Preacher. Lights and "court" change into "church" and Preacher and Cora crosses back to "store"* D. R.)

CROWD. Amen.

PREACHER. God forgive us.

CONGREGATION. Amen.

PREACHER. In your wisdom forgive us. And help these two souls, these two innocent souls forget that dark moment.

CONGREGATION. Amen, amen.

PREACHER. Blind them to that dark moment and set them free, Lord.

CONGREGATION. Amen.

PREACHER. Dear Lord.

CONGREGATION. Amen.

PREACHER. Our Savior! (*Lights fade on Preacher and Congre-*

19

gation, and up on "cafe." Walter crosses D. *from second platform* R. *of pole to* D. R.)

WALTER. (*In the cafe to Cora.*) Where do you want the pie?

CORA. (*Warmly chiding.*) On the rack that says pies.

WALTER. And the coffee in the jar that says coffee and the typed up menus in the menu covers? I'll catch on.

CORA. You're doing fine.

MARTHA. (*Standing* D. L. *facing* U.) A show place.

WALTER. Well, for only a week.

WILMA. (*Beside Martha.*) I hear.

CORA. You'll catch on.

WALTER. And you have to consider that we spend more time upstairs than down, or I'd know a lot more about the restaurant business and a lot less about you.

CORA. Now you just clam up before somebody comes in.

WALTER. Ashamed, are you?

CORA. No, I certainly am not and you know it, but I don't intend to bother someone else's business with my own.

WALTER. Wonder what they think?

CORA. You do do you?

WALTER. "No I most certainly do not and you know it"—I like the way you people talk. You're looking good.

CORA. I'm feeling good.

WALTER. (*Crosses* U. R. *to second platform.*) What would you think about putting an awning over the door so a fellow doesn't get soaking wet with rain as soon as he steps out the door.

CORA. Hm. What'd I care if he's going out?

WALTER. (*Crosses* D. R. *step and Walter and Cora sit on edge of second platform.*) Oh, it might be that on the way out is when he decides to come back.

CORA. You think, do you?

WALTER. "You think, do you?" It's something to consider.

WILMA. A show place. (*Martha and Wilma sit. Lights come up on upper top platform and the Johnson family "kitchen"—Mavis, followed by Patsy—*R.—L.)

PATSY. It's a trash heap is what it is. I don't know what keeps us here; I swear (*Dead pause. Evelyn crosses* D. L. *and sits beside Martha to have a lemonade break.*) I don't. Maybe it was all right when you were young. The only people who ever comes into town

20

is people to drive around looking around, poking around to see what a ghost town looks like. Movie house been closed down eight years; you want to see a movie you have to drive twenty miles into Centerville. Every building on Main Street closed up falling down except a store and a grubby filling station, boys stand out hanging around, it's a disgrace. (*Lights slowly come up on three women.*)

EVELYN. —Can't be healthy, rats took over the old grainery, all the buildings rotting and falling down, the mine shaft building used to just shine; you could see it miles away; now the way it sags— falling apart, boarded together; everything flapping and rusting, it's an absolute eye-sore. Cats poking around through the rotting ruins of all those old buildings, their bellies just busting, it can't be healthy.

PATSY. Dad could get a job in Centerville as well as here; I don't know why we stay here, there's a lot of decent people there, they know how to have fun, but no. We have to stay here. The boys from Centerville *all* have cars, I'm so ashamed getting off that ugly smelly school bus with all those younger kids, squealing; I swear sometimes I think I'm just going to sit there and not budge all day. Just let them drive right into the parking lot and sit there in the hot sun all day broiling rather than get off that bus with the boys all standing around the front of the school watching. I just wish you knew—they're probably surprised I don't smell of cow manure.

PECK. Patsy.

PATSY. Well, I'm sorry but it's true. I wish you could see the way they dress! In the summertime the boys from Centerville drive by on the highway along side the field and I'm up on the hay wagon like some common hired hand and they yell and honk and carry on so damn smart and I just wish I could die.

MAVIS. Patsy June.

PATSY. Well, I'm sorry but I do. At night sometimes I just cry my eyes out. Night after night. I just cry myself to sleep; I hope you're satisfied.

EVELYN. Trying to scratch a living together. Trying to keep strong.

PATSY. I'm sorry, but I do. (*Crosses c. on edge of second platform.*)

EVELYN. Sometimes I don't even know why we try. (*Light c. area.*)

LENA. (*Crosses from* D. R. C. *where she had crossed on from* U. L. *and crosses* U. C. *and sits beside Patsy on top platform edge.*) I said it's warm, for crying out loud; it's May; school's nearly out; I don't know why I have to wear that ugly old thing, you have the nicest clothes. I never have a danged thing.

PATSY. Well, all the boys were wearing cashmere sweaters with V necks and I said if they can have them I sure as hell can; the girls in my class just turned pea-green-purple. I said, well they didn't have what I wanted in Centerville, this two-bit town so I went along with dad to Des Moines, you should have seen them.

LENA. Peggy was furious.

PATSY. Oh, she thinks she's so rich, she has absolutely no taste at all.

LENA. I know.

PATSY. Black and brown and blue and green; I said the other day, why, Peggy, you look exactly the color of Chuck Melton's two-toned Mercury. You should have seen her face.

LENA. I wish I could have.

PATSY. Well, listen; Chuck thinks he's so damn smart himself. Yelling to me, you should hear the things they say. It'd make your ears burn. I told him and he should know, if he wants to come by and come up to the door and knock like some kind of respectable person, then I'd go out; but I'm not going to just fly out of the house like that. He thinks he's so damn smart, I don't care how long he sits out in front of the house in his damn car. Honking. He can honk all night for all I care. (*Lights fade on* C. *area and Wilma and Evelyn cross* U. L. *Lena crosses* D. L. *to mother.*)

MARTHA. Evelyn said a regular show place.

WILMA. I heard she closes up at ten every night now.

MARTHA. Oh my.

WILMA. Ours is not to judge.

MARTHA. Still I know what I know.

LENA. (*Both Martha and Lena look at dead "Blackie."*) I know he did it. Why would anyone want to poison Blackie? He's just a helpless dog.

MARTHA. He just looked up at me like he knew I'd help him and there wasn't anything I could do this time and I think he knew.

LENA. I don't understand somebody doing something like that.

MARTHA. There wasn't anything I could do. Just nothing at all.

LENA. Why?

MARTHA. I don't know, love. (*Lights down and up like blink of eye.*)

LENA. Why?

MARTHA. I don't know, love. (*Same as above.*)

LENA. Why?

MARTHA. I don't know love.

LENA. (*Picks up "dog."*) Just a helpless little dog, he was too old to hurt anybody. There's somebody poisoning dogs around here and that's the lowest, meanest thing in the world.

MARTHA. No one should cause an animal to suffer like that.

LENA. (*Crosses D. R. to bury "dog."*) I know he did it, too. I know it was him.

MARTHA. Well, we can think what we think, but we can't do anything.

LENA. I've seen how they bark at him; you know that. Blackie could tell an evil person; a dog can tell; they're all scared of him.

WILMA. (*Crosses D. L. C. beside Martha.*) Wickedest man; creeping through town, looking into things.

MARTHA. Peeping into girls' bedrooms; standing around looking like that.

WILMA. Who knows what's in someone's mind like that? (*Lights fade out on Martha and Wilma. Patsy screams very loud, running into the area, with her mother, father and Josh.*)

PECK. What in God's name?

PATSY. Oh, god, oh, god, oh, god, oh, god. In there.

MAVIS. What's wrong, baby?

PATSY. I saw him. I saw him. Oh, god, he was looking in the window. His face—

PECK. Who was? Answer me?

MAVIS. Skelly?

PATSY. Skelly. Skelly. Skelly was. Oh, god, you should have seen his eyes! And I was only in my pants. You should have seen him.

JOSH. I don't know what he could have seen.

MAVIS. That's enough out of you now.

PECK. Where was he?

PATSY. At my bedroom window, where do you think?

MAVIS. You're imagining things; you're dreaming.

PATSY. I wasn't sleep, I tell you; I just was getting ready for bed.

23

PECK. It's okay now, I'll go out. (*Begins to cross* R.)

PATSY. No, he's gone now, my god, I screamed and he ran away.

PECK. (*With some humor. Crosses back* U. C.) Well, I'd think he would.

JOSH. Wake the dead; what's he gonna see?

MAVIS. Don't you start.

PATSY. (*Contrite.*) I'm sorry.

MAVIS. For what?

JOSH. Sorry he didn't come on in probably.

PATSY. For scaring you so.

MAVIS. It's all right. My word, something like that, I'd think you would.

PATSY. Only I was just so scared.

MAVIS. Of course you would. (*Josh is stifling a laugh.*) That's enough dad said.

PATSY. It was horrible.

MAVIS. It's all right now.

PATSY. I don't think I can go back in my room.

JOSH. Oh, good Lord.

PECK. Young man.

MAVIS. It's all right now.

PATSY. Can't I sleep with you tonight?

MAVIS. It's all right now.

PATSY. Just tonight.

MAVIS. No, now, he's gone.

JOSH. What are you, some kind of baby?

PATSY. I was just so scared.

MAVIS. Go on back to bed, honey.

PATSY. I'm sorry.

MAVIS. It's okay.

PATSY. It was horrible. Can't I sleep between you? I'm shaking like a leaf.

MAVIS. It was nothing.

PATSY. Just tonight?

MAVIS. You're too big for that kind of thing.

PATSY. Something ought to be done about him.

MAVIS. It was nothing; it was your imagination, it was the wind; it was the shadows.

24

PATSY. It was Skelly Mannor! I guess I know him when I see him.

MAVIS. Go on back to bed. He's gone.

PATSY. I know I saw him.

MAVIS. Go on, it's Okay now; he's gone; whoever it was.

PATSY. Well, it was Skelly Mannor, I guess I know who it was, I saw him. (*Crosses down step and onto second platform* C. *Lookout "window."*)

MAVIS. Something ought to be done about him.

JOSH. He hasn't hurt anyone—not yet.

MAVIS. I suppose you call scaring an innocent girl out of her wits doing nothing. And the whole family too. Everyone knows what he does.

JOSH. Well, what could he do but look? He must be over a hundred if he's a day.

MAVIS. Just looking is doing; who knows what he might do?

JOSH. He's eighty years old.

PATSY. (*Crosses back* U. C. *into "kitchen."*) He is not. How can you tell how old he is, through all that filth.

PECK. Well, I know when I was a young man like Josh or younger we used to give old Skelly a Baaa sometimes—

MAVIS. Peck, now—

PECK. Well, and he looked the same then as he does now, and all the men then said he'd been looking like that for as long as they could remember so he's getting on.

JOSH. He's just a curiosity.

PATSY. Oh, that's very funny. A curiosity. You're just bright as the sun; you ought to hide your head under a barrel.

JOSH. He's not hurt anybody. Except Warren Peabody.

PATSY. Well, Warren Peabody deserved whatever he got, I'm sure.

MAVIS. What did he do to Warren, is that Laura Peabody's boy?

PATSY. Oh, lord no; you know he drives an old chevy, from over at Centerville; part of that river trash bunch. (*Patsy crosses* D. R. *to Lena and lights up on them and Martha and Wilma* D. L.)

JOSH. Well, he hit Warren in the back of the head with a rock, threw it, I'll bet thirty feet, caught Warren running, knocked him out cold.

LENA. (*Talking to Patsy.*) I remember when Driver was alive.

PATSY. Before his accident.

LENA. This was a wonderful place.

PECK. He's got a good aim, I can vouch for that.

MAVIS. I've told you, Josh, I don't want you boys teasing him. You just ignore him, I don't care how old you are. I don't know why you do that. You know he could turn on you any second.

JOSH. Oh, I don't bother him.

MAVIS. Well, who knows what's in somebody's mind like that.

WILMA. Like that time he scared young Patsy so bad.

MARTHA. Bad for the whole town with someone like that.

LENA. Like that parade every Saturday afternoon with Driver spinning through town, laughing; I remember his laugh.

PECK. I remember he let Curt Watson have it across the side of the face once. Curt was the fastest runner in town too; let him have it once when Curt gave him a Baaa.

JOSH. God knows he's crazy enough to try to do something like that with a sheep.

MAVIS. Josh, now.

JOSH. Well, I figure maybe he couldn't get a girl.

MAVIS. That's enough.

JOSH. Well, now; the whole town knows what he did; it's not like it was some secret—it's the funniest thing anyone's ever seen around here.

MAVIS. It's not our place to talk.

PECK. I don't imagine he did it much more than once and that time he got caught.

JOSH. That's about the dumbest thing I ever heard. He must have been really hard up is all I can say.

WILMA. (*Referring to dog's death.*) To do some bestial thing like that.

MARTHA. When I think of the evil in this world.

LENA. (*Referring to Driver's death.*) I could just cry.

JOSH. Who saw him?

PECK. Hell, I don't know. It must have been before I was born.

JOSH. Hell, he must be eighty years old.

PECK. Well, he's getting on.

PATSY. And Driver Junior. I think he hated his brother. He's just nothing compared. His brother was always so happy at least.

LENA. Driver's been dead now three years tomorrow.

PATSY. May thirtieth.

LENA. Every time I see that car; it just kills me.

JOSH. Some dumb old sheep herder. I hear they're all like that.

PECK. Well, they don't get into town much.

JOSH. Shit, I wish I could of seen him. That old son-of-a-bitch. We ought to have him tarred and feathered on Halloween if anyone could find him on Halloween. That old bastard, I don't know how he gets away with the things he does. I know Driver and me was gonna run him out of town once; I think we got drunk instead.

PECK. When was that?

JOSH. Just before his accident some time. Shit we used to run that old boy ragged.

PECK. You watch yourself.

MARTHA. When I think of the evil in this world, I swear.

LENA. I could just cry. (*Lights fade out on Patsy and Lena* D. R., *and Martha and Wilma* D. L.)

MAVIS. A decent person is afraid to move outside at night; now what kind of life is that?

PECK. Well, we'll tell Sheriff Clevis and see what he says. He can't do nothing; we didn't catch him at it.

MAVIS. It'll be too late one day and then who's to blame. (*Lights fade out on top platform and special comes up on Nelly sitting on* D. R. *edge of top platform.*)

MARY. (*Crosses* D. *to Nelly.*) I saw it.

NELLY. Sure you did, mama.

MARY. In my dream. Oh, god; it was horrible, Nelly.

NELLY. Go back to sleep mama.

MARY. Someone's going to be butchered in this town. Blood is going to be shed.

NELLY. Be still.

MARY. Blood is going to be shed; someone is going to be butchered.

NELLY. Go on out into your garden, mama; go back upstairs. (*Lights up on "church." Focus on Preacher and Congregation.*)

CONGREGATION. (*Softly singing.*) I walk through the garden alone; while the dew is still on the roses . . . (*Fading. Eva crosses* D. C. *from* U. L. *and Skelly crosses* C. *from* R.) And the voice I hear, falling on my ear—the prince of peace discloses . . . (*As Eva steps off top platform lights come up on* D. C. *and* D. R. C.)

SKELLY. Hey. (*Grabs Eva.*)

EVA. What? What? What do you want?

SKELLY. You tell him.

EVA. What? I don't know who you're talking about—what do you want?

SKELLY. Your friend.

EVA. Who?

SKELLY. Him. Robert.

EVA. Tell him what.

SKELLY. Tell him he's all right.

EVA. (*Breaks away from Skelly and begins to cross* U. C.—U. L.) What do you mean he's all right?

SKELLY. He's a good boy.

EVA. Well, I imagine he knows that.

SKELLY. (*Crosses* C.) People talk but they don't know—it's them that's the bastards. He's all right.

EVA. You're terrible the way you talk. Nobody makes fun of him —it's you they laugh at.

SKELLY. You tell him—

EVA. I don't know what you're talking about. I wouldn't tell anybody anything you told me to tell them. (*Eva crosses* U. L. *Skelly remains at* C. *Cora and Martha cross into "store," which is second platform, as lights fade* D. C. *and come up on "store."*)

CORA. He drifted in town and he helped around the cafe for awhile and he drifted on; nothing was holding him here.

MARTHA. I heard you started closing the place up at ten in the evening when that boy started working for you.

CORA. When Walter came, yes, I did. I closed earlier. I don't know why I used to be open all that late for anyway.

MARTHA. I heard you still close it up at ten though.

CORA. Well, force of habit, I suppose.

MARTHA. How long is it he's been gone?

CORA. I don't know, Mrs. Truit; I suppose a month now.

MARTHA. I heard you two made that cafe a regular show place.

CORA. You'll have to come up sometime and have a cup of coffee and a piece of pie.

MARTHA. Yes, when you was still with your husband, before he left, I mean, I know you used to make the best pie in the state.

CORA. It's still pretty good.

MARTHA. (*Crosses* D. L.) Yes, I will, I'll come up and see you one day. (*Cora crosses* D. R. *Lights out on "store" and up on Martha and Wilma* D. L. C.) "Helped around the store," did you ever hear anything like it? I heard she still closes the cafe at ten sharp. They say he left without taking so much as a stitch she'd bought him. Didn't leave a note even—

JOSH. (*Crosses to* D. R. *corner of top platform with trucker.*) I hear Hilltop would be an easy place to break into, if you had in mind to steal something.

MARTHA. Leaves the door for him still, every night.

WILMA. I hear.

MARTHA. Closes at ten.

TRUCKER. That's what I heard.

WILMA. (*Getting ready for church.*) What Reverend Parker said is so true.

MARTHA. Oh, I know it is.

WILMA. It's difficult for us to accept.

MARTHA. (*Skelly crosses to* R. *pole.*) "We must accept the blame upon ourselves. Each and every one of us."

WILMA. "It's not Nelly Windrod who is being tried here today."

MARTHA. Nelly Windrod is not the person who is being tried here today.

WILMA. —No indeed— (*Lights up on Congregation.*)

PREACHER. (*At* U. C.) —It is the sole responsibility of our very community. The laxity with which we met the obligations of our Christian lives. The blindness from which we allowed evil in our lives.

CONGREGATION. Amen.

PREACHER. Evil in our lives.

CONGREGATION. Amen.

PREACHER. We watched it fester and grow; we allowed this dreadful thing to happen through shirking our Christian duty. Nelly Windrod—

WILMA. Is not on trial here today.

PREACHER. —No indeed. That man. May the Lord have mercy on his soul. (*Waits.*)

29

CONGREGATION. Amen.

PREACHER. May the Lord have mercy on his soul and mercy on our blindness to his way. It is our responsibility and we must share in that terrible knowledge. (*Lights begin to fade on Congregation as Lena crosses* C., *and Patsy leans against post* D. L.)

LENA. It's not that bad.

PATSY. It's terrible, this crumby old ghost town; tumbleweed blowing down the deserted streets.

LENA. (*Crosses* D. C.) There's no tumbleweed blowing down the—

PATSY. (*As Patsy crosses* D. C. *lights there come up.*) Well, there ought to be, it's enough to give a person the creeps. Everyone from Centerville and all over driving by to see where the murder was committed; it's creepy. Looking at this awful ugly old ghost town, and all the boys know I live here, I swear, I've never been so humiliated in my life.

LENA. I know, it's terrible.

PATSY. Driver Junior never talks to anyone anymore— I haven't even seen him with Eva; of course her—that dumb cripple hasn't said a word since. Everyone staring at her—the whole thing is just the ugliest thing I ever heard about. I knew what was going to happen, I said. I swear Driver Junior is such a creep—never spoke to anyone in his life anyway. Doesn't hang around with us or anyone else his own age; hanging around with her, that girl, I feel sorry for her and all, but I look at her and I just feel my shoulderblades start to pooch out all over, people like that—deformed people ought to be put out of sight. Like her and Skelly and everybody; I mean people with deformed minds as well, too; don't think I'm forgetting that. It's absolutely creepy the way people drive through here; I've never been so humiliated in my life. (*Patsy crosses* U. R.—*Lena crosses* D. L. *Robert crosses* D. C.)

SKELLY. You! Hey, Robert. Bobby! Hey!

ROBERT. Hay is for sheep.

SKELLY. Yeah, uh, you, uh—Driver is dead.

ROBERT. Well, I guess I know that.

SKELLY. You going around like—

ROBERT. What? What do you want?

SKELLY. He was a son-of-a-bitch.

ROBERT. Don't talk like that to me.

SKELLY. You don't talk bad.

ROBERT. I don't, no, because I don't see any need to talk—
SKELLY. Driver was a sonabitch. Walking like some kind of stud horse. He wasn't human.
ROBERT. Who are you to tell if someone is human or—
SKELLY. You know what he did? I saw. You didn't go to the races to see him kill himself.
ROBERT. My brother was a very good race car driver and I didn't go because I don't like them, if everyone went and I didn't it's because they like them and I don't.
SKELLY. You don't know. I'll tell you what your sonabitch was like.
ROBERT. You don't know anything.
SKELLY. You hear me talking to people? I *see*. He was a snot nose kid twelve when you was born. I saw him. And him driving through town like a big shot. With his racing car all green and yellow and rared back there. Lined up after him in cars, trailing after him and honking like a string of geese coming into town.
WILMA. (*Over.*) Land, it was wonderful just to hear them cheering.
MARTHA. (*Over.*) Another silver cup, another blue ribbon.
WILMA. (*Over.*) First place.
SKELLY. And him telling everybody about it up at the cafe. I heard the stories and the shouting and the glory.
ROBERT. I don't know what you're talking about.
SKELLY. I saw him with Betty Atkins—in her bedroom and her crying and crying and how he hit her—you didn't know that! And she cried 'cause he got so mad. He liked to killed her.
ROBERT. I thought people made up stories about you peeping into windows—you're worse than they say.
SKELLY. I SAW HIM! You're better for a man than he is.
ROBERT. You're disgusting; you're as bad as everybody says you are. Dad says you are and Driver said so too.
SKELLY. Yeah, because I told him I saw him. Your brother you know what he did? You know what he did? He had to help himself. Had to help himself out. Out in his car parked on the road and in his room. He had to do it for himself.
ROBERT. Shut up!
SKELLY. That's what I know.

ROBERT. You're disgusting. You should be killed or jailed; my brother was a good person; he was a wonderful person.
SKELLY. He beat Betty Atkins and did it by hand. Jacking all on her. I've seen him. I've seen him.
ROBERT. Baaaaaaa.
SKELLY. That's what I know.
ROBERT. You're worse than they say. Everybody knows you can spy on them. Who do you think you are.
SKELLY. Who do you think your sonabitch brother was? Is what I want to—
ROBERT. Baaaaaaa. Baaaaaaa.
SKELLY. Now you know! Go on.
ROBERT. BAAAAAAAAA! Baaaaaaaaa.
SKELLY. Get on—get on—Driver Junior, you like that? I know, I know. You like that? Get on. Hey— (*Robert exits. Skelly freezes. Lights fade on Skelly and come up on Wilma and Martha D. L., as Eva crosses D. C. and recreates former scene with Skelly.*)
WILMA. When that boy died the heart of this town was buried with him.
MARTHA. It was wonderful.
WILMA. Gave of himself, gave of himself until there was nothing else and killed himself in an accident.
MARTHA. The Lord giveth and the Lord taketh away.
WILMA. Poor lad. I swear. (*Silence.*)
SKELLY. Boy! Robert! Boy! Hey!
EVA. What? What? What do you want?
SKELLY. You tell him—
EVA. What? I don't know who you're talking about—what do you want?
SKELLY. Your friend.
EVA. Who?
SKELLY. Him. Robert.
EVA. Tell him what?
SKELLY. Tell him he's all right.
EVA. What do you mean he's all right?
SKELLY. He's a good boy. (*As Skelly crosses C. take D. R. C. and C. lights out.*)
EVA. Well, I imagine he knows that.

SKELLY. People make fun of him—but they don't know—it's them that's the bastards. He's all right.

EVA. You're terrible the way you talk. Nobody makes fun of him. It's you they laugh at.

SKELLY. You tell him.

EVA. I don't know what you're talking about. I wouldn't tell anyone anything you told me to tell them.

SKELLY. You tell him . . . (*Lights up on trial as Peck crosses to* D. R. *corner of top platform and Nelly in "witness box."*)

PECK. We of the jury find Nelly Windrod. Not guilty.

NELLY. Oh, god, oh, god. Mama? (*All freeze, bump in special on Judge* U. C.)

PREACHER. It is not Nelly Windrod who is on trial here today. (*Lights bump out on Judge and bump up on Patsy in Nelly special, and Lena in special* D. L. *by post.*)

PATSY. Tumbleweed blowing through town, it's so creepy I don't know how anyone can stand it.

LENA. There's no tumbleweed blowing through . . . (*As Lena says line Eva and Mary cross to* C. *to platform and special comes up on them.*)

MARY. (*To Eva.*) You talk to little Robert and that's nice. I talk to things too. I talk. I have several tropical fish and a number of small birds that I feed each and every day and take excellent care of them. Talking with them until they die. I like little things, with little hearts beating and little lives around me. Their little hearts just moving away. With short life-spans and high temperatures. And I pat out little graves like loaves in the back yard and put little white-washed gravel, little rocks around each one and that's my garden. And I decorate the little loaves with flowers when I remember to. Now there's Trinket. That was my rat terrier, died eleven years ago last November, and Bonnie, my cocker spaniel, died four years ago last October, all in the Fall; and Gilda and Wanda the two goldfish; floating on their sides one morning, little loaves, those two. And Chee-chee, my canary, died two years ago last September. And Goldie, my other canary, passed on the year after that and Tina the little blue kitten; beautiful kitten, that one's little too. She prefers violets and Goldie takes daisies and Chee-chee takes dandelions and Bonnie takes roses, and Trinket has daffodils generally—spring daffodils and Wanda tulips; and the flowers dry up and die and I feel I should bury them too. All my children. Gone, gone, gone. (*Eva crosses* U. L. *by Evelyn. Mary crosses* D. *to Nelly on second platform. Lights up on Congregation keeping lights out on Cora's "cafe."*)

CONGREGATION. (*Singing softly.*) I walk in the garden alone. While the dew is still on the roses. And the voice I hear. Falling on my ear. The son of God discloses. And he walks with me— (*Lights up on "cafe." Cora crosses* D. R. C. *from* R. C. *of second platform.*)

CORA. (*Enters the cafe from "upstairs," sleepily, calling softly as wakened from sleep.*) Walter?

CONGREGATION. And he talks with me.

CORA. Walter?

CONGREGATION. And he tells me I am his own.

CORA. Walter?

CONGREGATION. And the joy we share.

CORA. Walter!

CONGREGATION. As we tarry there!

CORA. Walter!

CONGREGATION. None other. Has ever—

CORA. Walter.

CONGREGATION. Known.

PREACHER. Let us pray. (*Lights slowly fade out on Congregation and Cora.*)

CORA. (*Falling to her knees as though felled.*) OH, god. Oh, god. Oh, god. Oh, god. Oh, god. Oh, god. Oh, god. (*Lights out—cast clear stage and house lights up.*)

CURTAIN

ACT II

Cast enters, with Patsy and Lena going to c. When all are in place lights up on Patsy and Lena.

PATSY. (*To Lena.*) It wasn't really sudden. I knew he wanted to, he'd let on, you know, in little ways. He said would I mind not being in school; he'll graduate, of course, 'cause this is his last year—and I said would I *mind?*
LENA. That's just incredible; when's it going to be?
PATSY. We aren't messing around; he said two weeks from this Saturday. He didn't want to have a church wedding at first—you know how he is, and I said, Chuck Melton, if you think I'm going to just run off to a preacher and practically elope you got another think coming. So it'll be the First Presberterian of Centerville, but I want it to be just simple. I said I wanted a street length dress— I know but that's what I want and I'll have a veil, a little pill-box hat, I love those, and a veil and probably roses, if it's not too early for roses.
MARY. (*On top platform. Over.*) Bonnie? Here girl. Bonnie? Here kitty, kitty.
LENA. I'm just so surprised.
PATSY. Well, it wasn't really sudden, I knew he wanted to, he'd let on. I love the First Presberterian.
PREACHER. (*Light on Preacher. Over.*) Now you know I'm aware we all want to get this settled and go home and forget about it. (*Light out on Preacher.*)
PATSY. I only hope the trial and all is quieted down. That could just ruin it all.
LENA. Oh, it will be.
PATSY. It's a beautiful church.
LENA. I really love it; it's just beautiful.
PATSY. And my aunt's gonna give the bride's breakfast.
LENA. Aren't you excited?
PATSY. I imagine we'll live in Centerville. You know, till we have enough money to get a place or maybe move somewhere. Probably

right in town; there's a wonderful place over the barbershop, the Reganson one on the corner with windows on both sides that's been empty for weeks. I only hope someone doesn't beat us to it. I want to tell Chuck to put some money down on it. I don't want to live with his folks. I just can't stand them and I don't think they think too much of me either. They're so square and old-fashioned. They really are. They don't even smoke or believe in make-up or anything.

LENA. Chuck is wonderful, he really is. I'm just so surprised.

PATSY. (*Beginning to cry gently.*) He was so cute; he said would I mind not being in school next year, junior year and I said of course I'll miss my friends, but would I *mind*?

LENA. It's so beautiful. It's a beautiful church for a wedding.

PATSY. Isn't it?

LENA. Aren't you excited? What's wrong?

PATSY. Well, of course I am, silly.

LENA. I don't think Josh and me want to get married though until after I'm out of school.

PATSY. Oh, my god, you don't want to marry Josh. My Lord, I can't imagine it. You're not serious about him. Lord, he's so childish.

LENA. He isn't. He's six years older than you are. He's worked for two years.

PATSY. Well, I know, but you don't want to marry him. Age doesn't have anything to do with it. He's all right and he's sweet and all, but I mean to go to the show with and hold hands. I don't know how you can bear to ride into town in that garage tow-truck, though.

LENA. I drive it sometimes; it's not bad.

PATSY. Well, I know, but Josh! Lord, Lena, I've got so many things to do yet. You know the thing I think I like most about Chuck is that he's so clean and neat and all. The way he takes care of his Mercury. It's always like spanking new. (*Lights up on Robert in "witness stand" for one line.*)

ROBERT. And he took us by surprise. (*Lights out on Robert and on "cafe"* D. R.)

CORA. You seem uneasy.

WALTER. I'm not really.

CORA. I depend on you too much probably.

WALTER. Huh? No, nothing's wrong.

CORA. I've always had a dream, an idea, of maybe leaving here.

WALTER. You have?

CORA. Would you like that?

WALTER. And go where? Hawaii?

CORA. Well, no, not quite Hawaii? I don't know. It's sometimes somewhere and sometimes somewhere else. Somewhere. St. Louis maybe; Des Moines, Chicago. Anywhere.

WALTER. What would you do there?

CORA. The same, of course. Only a nice place maybe. I know the business, if I could sell this place.

WALTER. You wouldn't want to do that would you?

CORA. Wouldn't you like that? St. Louis maybe, or anywhere. I thought you'd like that. Have a bigger place. Maybe hire someone to run it for us so it doesn't take up all our time.

WALTER. That's an idea. I can't say I like St. Louis much.

CORA. Have you been there? Well, Chicago then.

WALTER. Chicago's nice.

CORA. I have a uncle in Chicago; he might help us get started. What's wrong, anything? You seem uneasy.

WALTER. I'm not. Why don't we close early.

CORA. I'd be agreeable to that. (*Lights out on "cafe" and up on top platform and* D. C.)

MARTHA. (D. L. *Then crosses to top platform with Patsy, Mavis, Evelyn, Wilma, Lena.*) Is she any better?

EVELYN. Oh, I don't know. Who can tell? (*Skelly crosses through ladies to* D. C. *As he steps off top platform, takes light off ladies on top platform.*)

SKELLY. (*Alone.*) Hound? Hey, hound. What are you shaking about, huh? I got a roast bone from Cora's for you. Here. (*Gives dog "bone."*) There you go. Go to it. Those guns scare you do they? Those hunters? Eh? You should have seen it with the mines running. With the mines working and the dynamite and the what-you-call-it booming around everywhere underground fifty times a day or more. Boom! That'd make you shake. (*Laughs.*) . . . Every hound in town kept out of sight from seven in the morning till seven at night. Under every bed in town. Eat it. That's roast bone. You. (*Laughs.*) Oh, hell, yes. They was fancy people; butter wouldn't melt. Old man Reiley bought the Eldritch place up on the hill, wouldn't no other place do for him and carried on with their miners drinking parties and societies if you please. And Glenna Ann sashaying around serving tidbits on a platter; oh, well to do. Blast all day in the mines all day and blast all night at home. Old Man Reiley called me every name in the book. Fit to be tied. She was a pretty one, too; only eighteen, the both of us her old man called me every name in the book. Chased me off the place with a crowbar. And we done it in the old man's wood shed. Oh, sure. I sneaks back the very same night and we done it out in the wood shed there. Everything smelling of hickory and cedar for their fancy fireplaces. Oh, yeah. And, oh, how she did squirm! Oh, lord. Saying to me, "Oh, I love you. Oh, I love you, oh, really I do, Skelly." Oh, shit. Till I thought she was gonna croak. Oh, Lord. Sashay around town. Never let on she even knew me. Glenna Ann. Pretty girl. Oh, yeah. No girl in town so pretty. Then or now. None in between. Don't you bury that. You eat that now. That's good. Old man Reiley moved off; she moved off, whole family, lock stock and petticoat. Mines give out, off they git. Oh, I love you so much. Oh, sure. Pretty girl too. Right in the wood house the very night her old man chased me off with a crowbar. (*Rises, crosses to post to get "pot of water."*) Playing in the shavings on the floor. Till morning, near. Sure. All blue. The bluest blue in the morning. Blue light on her gown there. Sticking her feet into the shavings—digging. Beautiful tits; no tits like that when or since. I guess you know Peck Johnson fairly beat the shit out of that girl of his last night. Whipped her good. Never seen anything like it. Patsy. Little whore she is, too. Nearly killed her. The old lady standing there watching, white as a ghost . . . Good! I say good! Whatever she done, I say good! She deserved it; little whore. Here, you whore. Go on with you! get on out with you. Filthy brother; whole family right along brother and sister both. She nearly bled. Thought he was gonna kill her. (*Crosses D. L. C.*) People don't care! What kind of thing goes on. What kind of devilment. Where'd you go to? Hound? What-are-you-not eating? That's a good girl. You're okay. Bluest blue you ever saw and her in a night gown; run right off of the house when I called up and off we went (*Reaches for "pot" U. R. Laughs.*) Oh, boy! Arms is no good. Can't lift 'em even over my head. Look a there. Red thing over her night gown there. Grass sticking to her feet. Barefoot. Right across the dew and all. (*Crosses* c.) That crippled girl, Jackson, she's got her leg shorter, one than the other. Cries. You never saw anything like it. Dances around her room in the window curtains, all lace, wrapped around her, dancing around like a banshee. Oh, he's all right. Tell him I said he's all right. Well, I guess he knows that. No, he don't know it, now, there! Better his no good brother. People don't care! They don't see. What. What they want to think they think; what they don't they don't. They don't care anyway; what kind of devilment. What goes on. Her old man, old man Reiley; never did know. No, no. Never did know. I weren't the only one either you can bet. Get some water boiling; (*Lights "fire"* c.) make some sassafras; good for the stomach. Cedar. All in the air. Bluest blue in the air. Hickory and cedar cedar cedar cedar cedar in the air. Sang. (*Crosses to* R. *post. Laughs.*) All manner of songs there. Soft so's it wouldn't carry to the house there. Carrying on, biting, (*Sits.*) thought she was gonna croak. Oh, really, Oh, I love you so! (*Laughs.*) Pretty girl. Beautiful tits. Beautiful tits. Oh, yes. (*Leans on post.*) Oh, sure. (*Lights out on Skelly, up on top platform.*)

MARTHA. Is she any better?

EVELYN. Oh, I don't know. Who can tell?

MAVIS. Has she said anything?

EVELYN. The doctor said it was just shock.

MARTHA. Well, I'd think so.

WILMA. I've never heard anything like it.

MARTHA. Like when he scared young Patsy so bad.

WILMA. Bad for the whole town.

MAVIS. It's awful.

PATSY. I feel so sorry for her.

WILMA. How's Driver Junior?

EVELYN. He hasn't been over. I don't know what to think about that. I'd told her not to go off; well, I won't say anything.

MARTHA. Such a shock. For us all.

MAVIS. A terrible thing.

EVELYN. She's always been so easily upset.

LENA. Well, she has cause.

PATSY. I just wish he was still alive! That's what I wish.

WILMA. When I think of the evil in this world.

EVELYN. The doctor said she just needs rest.

39

MAVIS. If he'd of lived he'd not have seen the light of day tomorrow.

WILMA. That poor girl.

MARTHA. (*Martha and Wilma cross* D. L.) And Nelly, that poor woman, the life that woman leads.

WILMA. I said to Eva's mother—

MARTHA. I know.

WILMA. Cried the whole time—

MARTHA. I saw.

WILMA. Only God in his heaven. (*Lights change to "court room" and Mary in "witness box."*)

MARY. It appeared to me that both the men were hitting at her. (*Tremendous crowd reaction.*)

JUDGE. Order!

MARY. It appeared to me.

JUDGE. Now you have testified, as a witness, Mrs. Windrod.

MARY. I was at my window, watching the moon.

ROBERT. Was there a moon.

MARY. A crescent moon that night, I know for sure.

JUDGE. You have testified that you saw—

MARY. Blood, everywhere; all over. It was terrible. On the porch, rivers and I was mopping and it spread with the water, all around, all over.

JUDGE. Driver Junior and young Eva clearly.

MARY. I didn't say clearly, I couldn't see clearly; I don't see well.

JUDGE. You testified you saw—

MARY. In my dream.

JUDGE. You were asleep?

MARY. Weeks ago and I told Nelly that blood was going to be shed, and I was wiping and it spread with the water, all around on the porch. (*Lights fade—then up again.*)

NELLY. And mama said someone was in the back yard and I took up the gun that I keep by the door, the shotgun; and checked to see if it was loaded and it was and I opened the door. (*Lights out on "court" and up on "cafe."*)

MARY. (*Over.*) Bonnie? Here kitty, kitty, here girl.

CORA. Did you go into town.

WALTER. Yeah.

CORA. Into Centerville?

WALTER. No, no, only into Eldritch.

CORA. Did you? Well, what do you think?

WALTER. Well, what can I tell you, it's a ghost town.

CORA. I told you.

WALTER. What was that big building?

CORA. The movie house?

WALTER. On the corner.

CORA. Oh, there was a drug store, and an exchange. And a lawyer's office and a couple of doctors up above had their office in that building. A dentist I think. That was the first building to shut down.

WALTER. Some people said hello like they knew me.

CORA. Well, they do know you from here.

WALTER. Wonder what they think?

CORA. You do do you?

WALTER. Sometimes.

CORA. Peck Johnson said the new boy "helping" me appeared to be a genuine good worker.

WALTER. What did you say to that?

CORA. Well, I said, oh, yes, yes, he's a genuine good worker.

WALTER. (*Laughing.*) I like some of them all right. The truck drivers are all right anyway.

CORA. Oh, they're from all over; they support the place. Have for years.

WALTER. Some of the people from Eldritch aren't so bad.

CORA. I think a couple of the girls have a crush on you. Well, I don't blame them.

WALTER. They're young.

CORA. Well, they're not all that damn young.

WALTER. It's gonna be a nice night.

CORA. It's gonna be a nice summer. (*Lights fade and next three lines are said in dim light.*)

EVA. No, in the wintertime and in the autumn especially. It's so nice; it smells so clean.

ROBERT. He came from nowhere!

EVELYN. (*In a burst.*) I said she shouldn't be out gone from the house like that! (*Lights up* D. R. C. *on Skelly as Josh and trucker cross* D. *Josh crosses to* R. *of Skelly and trucker crosses to* L. *of Skelly—Skelly standing by* R. *post.*)

JOSH. What are you standing on the corner about? Why aren't you back to your grubby house? Where do you sleep now your stinking shack burned down? Or do you sleep? Do you sleep? Sleep with sheep, huh?

SKELLY. Get on.

JOSH. What'd you say?

SKELLY. Mind your own business.

JOSH. Which old damp rotting cellar do you haul up in now your dry old shack's gone? Huh? I bet you eat worms, doncha.

SKELLY. Go on you.

JOSH. What'd you eat? Won't tell anybody where you live will you? 'Cause you know what'd happen if you closed your eyes there don't you?

SKELLY. Yeah, you sonabitch, you mind your own—I don't say whether I got ary a bed or no now.

JOSH. What'd you call me?

SKELLY. Go on with you.

JOSH. I said what'd you call me?

TRUCKER. Ought to kill him, Josh.

JOSH. What'd you say? Shit he ain't worth it.

SKELLY. (*Crosses* U. C.) Get on.

JOSH. (*Josh and trucker follow* U. C.) Just don't let anybody follow you home. (*Skelly leaves.*) You get on now. You're the one who had better get on, not me. You'll wake up to a hot bed one of these days again. (*Laughs.*) Old bastard. BAAAAA! (*Laughs.*)

TRUCKER. Son of a bitch shepherd. (*Lights up on "court." Robert in "witness box."*)

ROBERT. He was just there all of a sudden from nowhere and he took us by surprise and he pushed me—he hit me from behind; I don't know if I passed out or not. (*All motionless except Nelly and Mary—lights like blink of eye out on "court" and on them* U. R. C.)

MARY. Nelly, Nelly, there's someone out back, honey, having a terrible fight. They came through the woods and started yelling all kinds of things.

NELLY. Where was you? I thought you was in bed.

MARY. You better go out and see honey. (*Blink of eye and lights back in "court." All watch and in scene.*)

ROBERT. He's immensely strong. (*Blink of eye and lights out on*

42

"court" and specials up on Patsy and Lena R. and L. of top platform.)

PATSY. I mean he's out there day and night polishing the chrome. The dash and all.

LENA. I know, it's amazing. (*Lights out on Patsy and Lena and up on "court."*)

ROBERT. And I heard a ringing in my ears and I saw what he was trying to do and everything went white. And he pushed me.

EVA. (*Crosses L. C. top platform and Evelyn holds her. A hugely ear-splittingly loud scream.*) AHHHHHHHHHHHHHHHH! AHHHHHHHHHHHHHH! AHHHHHHHHHHHH!

EVELYN. Oh, god, baby, my baby.

EVA. No, no, no, no, no!

EVELYN. See her crippled body. See her broken back; why, why has God crushed me with this burden. I don't complain. I ask why? We love Him. We bless Him. Praise Him. And this monster! I mean Skelly! My daughter is weak; you're trying to kill her! Look at her! Is that what you want? I only ask why?

PREACHER. The Lord works in—

EVELYN. (*Cora crosses into "witness box." Over.*) WHY? I said, Why? I have a right to know; I'll repent if I've done anything; if I've sinned.

CORA. (*Over.*) Eva said to me—Eva you know what you said. Skelly worked for me sometimes; none of you knew him. He was honest.

EVELYN. (*Overlapping. Evelyn crosses one step closer to "witness box" still on top platform. and Eva crosses U. L. of mother.*) My daughter has never spoken to you; my daughter has never spoken to a person like you; my daughter has been scarred, permanently scarred by this. She's crippled already. She's weak. She can't stand up.

CORA. If you'd listen to me.

EVELYN. No, no. I won't listen to you; I won't trust the word of a woman like you.

CORA. And what are you?

EVELYN. My daughter is a virgin! She's pure! She's a Christian, from a Christian home; a daughter of God and you'd put your word against the word of a virgin. A beer swilling harlot. Everyone knows. A drunken whore of Babylon!

43

CORA. I talked to her because I knew Skelly would never. Never harm anyone.

EVELYN. (*Riding over.*) Harlot! Daughter of Babylon! Go back to your beer parlor; your house of sin. You couldn't keep your husband and you couldn't keep your whore boy friend. In the name of God.

JUDGE. Order. Order. Order. Order. (*Begins pounding steadily with the "gavel."*)

EVELYN. In the name of God, before this court you know what I call you? You liar? Before God! (*Lights change to Congregation. The Congregation begins to sing "When the Roll is Called Up Yonder," to the rhythm of the steady gavel.*) [*Note: Words of hymn given at back of book.*] I won't let you call my daughter a liar. You're the liar. Before God I call you that. On His word. His holy word. Yes! Put her on the stand. Let her talk, we have nothing to hide. Ask her if she didn't keep a whore boy friend up to her place. (*Cora crosses to* D. R. *step.*) Ask her what kind of a woman she is . . . (*Evelyn crosses back* U. L. *and into Congregation singing. The Congregation drowns her out with the loud joyous hymn, the pulpit beaten now, in time to the song. The song is sung to its finish. Silence. Everyone moves into small groups. Worried, silent, Judge, Peck, Trucker and Josh cross* C. *and sit. Eva crosses* D. R. C. *and sits. Lights out on Congregation and up on Patsy and Walter in "witness box."*)

PATSY. Pretty sure.

WALTER. (*Pause.*) Are you sure it's me? (*Pause.*) You're not sure are you? (*Pause.*) It could be somebody else. It could have been what's-his-name. Chuck. (*Pause.*)

PATSY. Well, it was somebody! (*Pause.*) Oh, God.

WALTER. I don't know what you want from me.

PATSY. I'll tell your precious Cora what you're like. Then we'll see how high and mighty you think you are. No, you wouldn't like that very much, would you? (*Patsy crosses* U. R. *Walter crosses to post. Lights out on second platform and up on four men* C.)

JUDGE. The oats was late 'cause the Spring was so wet.

PECK. Me and the boy couldn't plant till the eighteenth of May. Up till then the ground was so wet we couldn't get at the field even.

TRUCKER. And then that cold spell.

JUDGE. Ground was solid out our way till almost April. You couldn't stick a fork into it. Hard as a rock.

PECK. 'Course you're high; it wasn't near so bad along in the valley.

TRUCKER. Oh, no. It wasn't near.

PECK. I don't imagine there was more than six-ten cold days. River wasn't more than three inches ice.

JOSH. I don't believe it ever froze clear across.

PECK. No, it never froze across.

JOSH. There was some running out a ways right through the winter.

PECK. 'Course you're up on the hill there. You're not protected.

JUDGE. 'Course the rains was bad for you. In the valley there.

JOSH. Oh, yeah.

TRUCKER. I don't believe I've ever seen the rains so bad.

PECK. Yeah, the river swelled up there along in March. I said to Josh, I couldn't remember it that bad.

JOSH. Most of the field was under six-ten feet of water along in the spring.

PECK. Wasn't able to set a plow till late in the month. Eighteenth of May; that's the latest I can remember. I believe it was the eighteenth.

JOSH. It was, I remember.

PECK. Latest I remember.

JUDGE. Well, you're in the valley there; you're not protected.

TRUCKER. The floods was bad for you.

PECK. It's rich soil, though. Good bottom topsoil.

TRUCKER. Yeah, it's rich bottom land.

PECK. It's good bottom land.

JUDGE. It's sandy for oats though.

JOSH. Yeah, the oats isn't doing well.

TRUCKER. Well, it's been dry the past month.

PECK. Radio says we might be heading for a drought.

JOSH. Yeah, we had all our rains right there together.

TRUCKER. Not what you'd call a deep rain though.

JUDGE. No, it run right off, much as there was of it. (*Stands.*) Could sure use some of it now.

PECK. Course you're up on the hill. You must be getting the worst

of it. (*Lights out on men* C., *and up on* D. L. *area. Judge crosses* U.
C., *Josh and Lena cross* D. L., *Patsy crosses* D. R. *Wilma and Martha
have crossed* L. *and* U. L. *on* D. L. *area to clear for kids. Cora and
Walter on second platform, backs to audience.*)

JOSH. Just got off work.

LENA. (*Finishing "make-up."*) You look it; you didn't even wash
up.

JOSH. I did, but it'll have to wear off; it's ground right in I think.

LENA. Where did you want to go tonight?

JOSH. You mind eating up at Cora's or you want to go into Centerville?

LENA. It doesn't matter, whatever you want.

JOSH. We might as well go on into town to the drive-in.

LENA. Oh let's, 'cause Patsy'll be there and I wanted to see her.

JOSH. You've seen her this morning.

LENA. Yes, but she said she had a surprise she wanted to tell me.

JOSH. I don't know what she thinks is a surprise. Then we'll go
into the movies, all right? Or would you rather just drive?

LENA. (*Crosses* L. C.) I'd kinda like to see the picture.

JOSH. Whatever you want.

LENA. She's gonna be with Chuck so you be nice to him. (*Lights
out* D. L., *up* D. R. *Lena crosses* D. R. *to Patsy. Josh crosses* C.)

PATSY. Don't you think he's cute though?

LENA. I guess.

PATSY. Was he really at the drive-in with you? That's so funny.
His name's Walter I found out. But I can't imagine. That's the funniest thing; I just wish I'd have seen it.

LENA. It's not so bad.

PATSY. But she's so old for him. My God she's thirty-eight.

LENA. She isn't is she? Mama said thirty-four.

PATSY. Well, she's older than any thirty-four and besides that's
bad enough.

LENA. That soldier you went out with last year was that old.

PATSY. He was not.

LENA. I'll bet he was. He was balding.

PATSY. He was not, what do you think I am, he had a crew cut;
besides he was twenty-six, I saw his ID.

LENA. Oh, he wasn't any twenty-six.

PATSY. I saw his draft card Lena. Besides, My God, it's different

46

with a boy. He was very nice. Besides I only went out with him twice. I felt sorry for him. We didn't do anything. (*Lights out* D. R. *and* D. R. C.—*Cora on edge of second platform—Eva* D. R. C.)

CORA. That's hard for me to believe, Eva.

EVA. You ask Robert; what difference does it make?

CORA. Cause he worked for me; he used to pick up the garbage for his hogs. He lived out back of the cafe for years, till they burned that shack down, I still say it was Driver Junior's brother and Josh did it, burned that shack down.

EVA. We come into the clearing back behind Nelly Windrod's house, by her mill there and I heard something and he said he'd show me what.

CORA. Skelly did? He did not.

EVA. No. He didn't say.

CORA. Eva if that's not the truth, you better say how it really happened.

EVA. (*Stands.*) I said it happened like Robert said. It's like that and I don't care if you knew him or not. Mama said the preacher said a sermon about (*Lights out* D. R. C. *Eva crosses to second platform. Cora stops her.*) the evil in people like him and that we should have killed him or something before he had a chance to take advantage of me. I've been cursed and scarred.

CORA. You can't lie under oath, Eva.

EVA. (*Crosses* U. L.) You're the one who's going to hell. Not me. I didn't do it, anyway; Nelly did it. (*Lights up on "court room"—Cora in "witness box."*)

CORA. It wasn't Skelly.

TRUCKER. Well, who do you think it was?

CORA. She told me.

MAVIS. Well, if he'd of lived, he wouldn't have seen the light of day tomorrow. (*Lights out on "court" and up* D. L. C. *on Josh and trucker looking at Martha* D. L. *playing with "Blackie."*)

JOSH. (*Almost good-naturedly.*) Damn that mutt anyway.

TRUCKER. Good watch dog is he?

JOSH. That old bitch of a dog, I'll kill that bitch.

TRUCKER. Wakes up the folks does he?

JOSH. Every damn time we drive up it starts up a racket. Son-of-a-bitch, every light in the house goes on. She has to run on in, the noise that dog raises, every goddamned night. I don't care how

47

easy I drive up. (*Josh crosses* U. R. *Trucker crosses* L. C. *of Peck.*) We started parking on down the block, she still starts up as soon as Lena steps a foot on the porch. (*Wilma crosses* D. L. *to Martha. Both standing over dead "dog.*")

MARTHA. When I think of the evil in this world.

WILMA. To do some bestial thing like that. (*Lights out* D. L. *and up* C. *as Judge crosses* D. *to Peck and trucker.*)

PECK. Well, I never figured him to actually hurt anybody.

TRUCKER. Hell, we all know he was looney.

JUDGE. Someone like that we all knew he was capable of any kind of thing.

PECK. Capable yes, but I never figgered him for actually hurting anybody.

TRUCKER. Well when somebody lives like that—away from everybody.

PECK. The boys give him a hard time but he can take care of himself.

TRUCKER. Should have been put away the way he looks at everybody.

JUDGE. Should have been shot—just shot in the woods; nobody the wiser.

PECK. I just never really figgered him to do anything. Capable yes, but I have to admit I'd never thought he'd do anything. Outright, I mean. (*Judge crosses* U. C. *Peck and trucker cross* U. R. *Lights out* C., *up* D. L. *as Martha and Wilma sit and look at "cafe."*)

MARTHA. Why, she called Evelyn Jackson a liar to her face, and Eva too. Swore things, the devil and his angels wouldn't believe it. She'd stand up there and swear black was white. (*Lights out* D. L. *and up on Mary and Nelly* R. C. *top platform.*)

MARY. Nelly, Nelly, there's someone out back, honey, having a terrible fight; they came through the woods and started yelling all kinds of things.

NELLY. Where was you? I thought you was in bed.

MARY. You better go out and see honey. (*Nelly crosses* D. *second platform to post—followed by Mavis from* U. R. *steps as lights out on top platform and up on second platform* C. *"witness box" area.*)

MAVIS. Morning.

48

NELLY. Good morning.

MAVIS. We don't see you to talk to much.

NELLY. Well, September is a busy time; I'm still saving up strength for Peck's corn crop this year.

MAVIS. It's sure looking good.

NELLY. I drive past; I've been keeping my eye on it.

MAVIS. How is the mill?

NELLY. Well, September is always good.

MAVIS. We see you drive by.

NELLY. Evenings I've been going into Centerville; talking to the farmers over there; say we might be into a drought.

MAVIS. We saw you, I believe going into the movie house there.

NELLY. Yes, I don't get a chance to go often.

MAVIS. Well, we don't go.

NELLY. I've seen the girl there.

MAVIS. Patsy? Oh, yes, Patsy enjoys it. She goes with Chuck; awfully nice boy; I guess you know we're planning a wedding; I said it wasn't any use having a church wedding, all amounts to the same—Patsy wouldn't hear of it, of course, so I suppose we're going all out.

NELLY. He's an awfully nice boy, I hear.

MAVIS. Do you? I'm glad to hear it; we hardly know them really; but he does seem sweet; his family has a lovely farm, we visited. Last Sunday. They grow up so fast.

NELLY. Quite a nice young lady.

MAVIS. We're proud of her. How's your mother?

NELLY. Oh, mom's the same; her mind's gone. I hate to leave her alone nights. Just like a child.

MAVIS. Well, you have a life of your own; you have to get out.

NELLY. Yes, I do. I hate to leave her though just the same.

MAVIS. We see you driving into Centerville.

NELLY. It's good to get away from the mill; Duane nearly runs it for me now.

MAVIS. I was talking to your mother; poor thing.

NELLY. Yes, it's sad.

MAVIS. I remember she had a fine mind.

NELLY. Yes, she did. One of the first registered nurses in Des Moines. Long time ago now; when she was a girl.

MAVIS. She goes on terrible about you; poor thing.

NELLY. I know, she doesn't know what she's saying half the time.

MAVIS. Still she tells things; it must be terrible for you.

NELLY. I'll take care of her, Mavis, as long as my strength holds out.

MAVIS. Martha Truit said, the life you have to bear.

NELLY. It's my cross, Mavis.

MAVIS. (*Crosses* U. *to top platform. Nelly follows.*) I know, I told Peck . . .

NELLY. How is Peck?

MAVIS. Oh, he's all right; his back is giving him trouble again. It's just nerves I keep telling him, but I don't know. Between you and me I don't know. (*Lights fade into "forest." People move into positions like "trees."*)

WILMA. Who knows what's in somebody's mind like that.

MARTHA. Like that time when was it, last summer.

EVA. (*Crosses to Robert* U. L.) No, in the winter time and in the autumn. It's so nice, it smells so clean.

ROBERT. (*Circles Judge, Eva following.*) Okay, the fall then.

EVA. (*Stops.*) Yes. And it's heavy, heavy frost and it covers everything and that's rime. (*Moves.*)

ROBERT. (*Circles Nelly.*) And it's just frost? Is it a hoarfrost?

EVA. That's it, hoarfrost is rime. And it covers everything. (*Circles Judge.*) Every little blade of grass and every tree and houses and everything. Like it's been dipped in water and then in sugar.

ROBERT. (*Circles Nelly.*) Or salt. Yeah, I know what it is.

EVA. It's better than ice storms or anything like that. And everything is white and sparkling so clean when the sun comes up it nearly blinds you and it's rare! (*Robert crosses* D. R. *to post.*) It doesn't happen every year. And that's what I'd like to be. What I'd like to do. I have a book with a picture of Jack Frost painting rime on a window pane with a paint brush. (*Eva crosses* D. R. *of Lena to Robert.*) Do you fly? Do you dream you fly?

ROBERT. When?

EVA. Ever?

ROBERT. I guess. I haven't thought about it. (*Crosses* C.)

EVA. How high? Think about it. It's important. Everybody flies, it's important how high.

ROBERT. I don't know. Just over the ground.

EVA. Really?

ROBERT. I guess. As high as my head. I'm always getting tangled up in wires and all. (*Sits* C. *on edge of top platform.*)

EVA. I'm way over the tree tops, just over the tree tops, just brushing against the tree tops, and I fly right over them, just brush them with my arms out. Over the whole town like an airplane. Spreading this salt frost in the autumn. I love autumn. And when the sun comes—

ROBERT. Right.

EVA. It'll blind you!

ROBERT. I've seen it.

EVA. It's so bright it blinds you. I want to fly like that, all over the town, right over everybody. It's beautiful. (*Skelly moves behind Judge from* U. C.) Listen. Listen. Did you hear something? (*Eva sits edge of second platform, "forest." Light out—lights up on cafe and* D. C. *as Cora sits on second platform near post—Walter* D. R. *Skelly crosses* D. C.)

CORA. Are you out there?

SKELLY. Here. Yeah.

CORA. Can Walter help you, you know Walter.

SKELLY. Yeah, I know.

CORA. We're gonna be turning in, but he can help you with it.

SKELLY. The white one, with the spots?!

CORA. Spotty?

SKELLY. Had a litter.

CORA. She did?

SKELLY. She had four but she ate one.

CORA. Skelly you just let them go wild, that's terrible; you should take them away from her.

SKELLY. The runt, the last one.

WALTER. She what? She ate one of them?

CORA. Pigs do that sometimes; they're terrible. A runt or something that they think is weak, they will.

WALTER. Couldn't you stop her?

SKELLY. I didn't see it.

CORA. Oh, he lets them just go wild, you can't get near them, one of them's all right, the brown one.

SKELLY. She's good.

CORA. One of them is tame and nice, the rest you can't get near

51

them. He has four. So that makes seven now, doesn't it? You're getting to be a regular rancher.

SKELLY. The brown's a good one.

CORA. (*Crosses* U. R. *second platform.*) He has an old hound dog he keeps too, he's good with them but they just run wild.

WALTER. You want me to help you?

SKELLY. I'm all right. You like her?

WALTER. Do I like? What? Who?

SKELLY. Johnson. (*Pause.*) That Patsy Johnson. Cora ain't good to you?

WALTER. Cora? I imagine she's good to everybody.

SKELLY. But you. She's good to you. I seen you with Patsy Johnson. You like her? You like that carrying on?

WALTER. What? I thought you were talking about your brown sow, I've not seen her.

SKELLY. I said, if you think you're a big man and you play around here and you play around there.

WALTER. You want me to help you slop the hogs?

SKELLY. I'll be all right.

WALTER. Well, if you make it your business to know what everybody is doing, I see why Cora makes sure we pull down the shades at night, and turn off the light and listen to hear if anyone's about. If that's your business I guess I don't have to tell you what Patsy Johnson is like.

SKELLY. She's a bitch.

WALTER. Patsy? And them that lies down with . . .

SKELLY. Cora's a good woman.

WALTER. Yes, well you slop the hogs and carry off the garbage and I build the fence and paint the cafe; we're none of us freeloaders I don't suppose. I don't imagine I owe anyone anything except money. I don't owe anybody time. I can't say I see it as any of your business anyway, Skelly. You don't have to worry about her, she's managed seven years without you or me either. Don't you think? (*Pause.*) Wouldn't you say? (*Pause.*) You go on and slop your hogs. (*Pause.*) Go on, get on, be thankful she gives it to you for the price of carrying it away. (*Pause.*) Hey. What do you do with those hogs anyway? How come they're so wild?

SKELLY. I feed 'em they run wild.

WALTER. Go on, I didn't mean anything by it. Good night. (*Walter crosses* R. *Skelly crosses* U. C. *Josh and Lena sit on* U. R. *second platform. Lights out* D. C. *and* D. R. *and up on top platform on Mary and Mavis.*)

MARY. I have a bruise there on the inside of my elbow, she holds on to me there, she pushes at me terrible, she can't help it. (*Lights out on top platform, up on* C. *and* D. C. *on Eva and Robert.*)

EVA. If you had a car you could drive all over.

ROBERT. What do I want with a car?

EVA. Are you afraid?

ROBERT. What for, so I can drive around the square. Around the square, around the square. It's all they ever do; all the boys with cars. Around the square and over into Centerville to a drive-in to eat and a drive-in to see a movie.

EVA. You just don't want to be like—

ROBERT. Everybody doesn't have to have a car. Everybody talks like that's all there is. The guys at school spend their whole lives in or on top of or under their cars. They eat in them and sleep in them and change clothes and drink and get sick and vomit and make out with their girls—it's all they even ever talk about. Evolution's gonna take their feet right away from them. Make turtles with wheels for legs out of them.

EVA. I think you're just afraid 'cause of Driver.

ROBERT. Well, that's another thing I hadn't thought of. They die in them too. Live and die without ever stepping outside. Why would I want that? (*Eva lies down on* C. *area of second platform. Lights fade out on stage leaving glow on Eva and Lena and Josh in dimness* U. R.)

LENA. Sometimes I think life is so short and we should enjoy it for the time we're here and then I think I should work really hard so I can be comfortable, you know, after I've made some money, and then I think how awful working all that time would be and most of my life would be gone by that time and I'd have wasted it, you know what I mean? No, no, don't, Josh!

JOSH. You said you would.

LENA. Sometime, I said.

JOSH. You don't want to?

LENA. It isn't that. You know. Don't now!

JOSH. What?

LENA. You know. (*Sigh. Bored, as though by rote.*) If something happens, you don't know what can happen. And there's no assurance of what can happen.

JOSH. Nothing can happen, I told you.

LENA. Come on. Don't now! I'm not kidding now.

JOSH. Just see.

LENA. You don't like me really or you'd respect me.

JOSH. What? I don't like you? Why do you think I want to?

LENA. You know what I mean.

JOSH. Just see. Just see. Just see. Nothing will happen; just see.

LENA. No, I said, now. Come on.

JOSH. Jesus Christ, Lena.

LENA. Well, don't be mad.

JOSH. Well, you let me go so far and then say no, I don't know what you expect.

LENA. It's all right, isn't it? (*Pause.*) Josh? (*Pause.*) Well, don't just sit there. (*Pause.*) I said sometime. (*Pause.*) Sometime, really. I mean it. (*Pause.*) Just not tonight. Okay? (*Pause.*) I want to, too, I just said not tonight. Really. (*Pause.*) It just scares me. Okay? (*Pause.*) Okay? (*Rapidly.*) Josh! Damnit, now, come on. No! I said and that means no! Good Lord. (*Beat.*) Now you're mad, aren't you? (*Lights up on Congregation.*)

PREACHER. No sir, it is the sole responsibility of our very community. The laxity with which we met the obligations of our Christian lives. The blindness from which we allowed Evil in our lives. We watched it fester and grow; we allowed this dreadful thing to happen through shirking our Christian duty. Nelly Windrod is not on trial here today. That man, may the Lord have mercy on his soul damned eternally to hell, and our blindness to his way. It is our responsibility and we must share that terrible knowledge. As you go your ways tonight. As you leave and walk and drive to your homes, realize that the burden must be ours and ask the Lord for his grace. Pray for these two souls as you pray for the lost, the outcast, as you pray for the soul of the damned, and the care of our boys overseas. Pray to the Lord to unlock the bitterness in the hearts of those like him in the world today and pray that they may see the light of His Holy way.

CONGREGATION. Amen.

PREACHER. Amen, the Lord be with you. (*Lights brighten like outside of church and everyone moves, ending in "tree" positions.*)
JOSH. (U. R. *second platform.*) Had the Olds out last night.
TRUCKER. The old man's Olds?
JOSH. Took it out onto the Old Sparta road and opened it up.
TRUCKER. Gene was out there last week.
JOSH. Pegged it. Hundred twenty. That old needle was bouncing against the peg and half the way back again. Two miles or over, then I eased it down. (*Lights change back into "forest." Pick up same positions.*)
TRUCKER. We'll have to take 'er out Sunday.
EVA. And it covers everything and that's rime.
ROBERT. And it's just frost? Is it a hoarfrost? (*Stops.*)
EVA. That's it, hoarfrost is rime. And it covers everything. Every little blade of grass and every tree and houses and everything. Like it's been dipped in water and then in sugar.
ROBERT. Or salt. I've seen it.
EVA. It's better than ice storms or anything like that. And everything is white and sparkling so clean when the sun comes up it nearly blinds you and it's rare, it doesn't happen every year. And that's what I'd like to be. What I'd like to do. I have a book with a picture of Jack Frost painting rime on a window pane with a paint brush. Do you fly? Do you dream you fly?
ROBERT. When?
EVA. Ever?
ROBERT. I guess. I haven't thought about it. (*They walk about the "forest," walking slowly through the people.*)
EVA. How high? Think about it. It's important. Everybody flies, it's important how high.
ROBERT. I don't know. Just over the ground.
EVA. Really?
ROBERT. I guess. As high as my head. I'm always getting tangled up in wires and all.
EVA. I'm way over the tree tops, just over the tree tops, just brushing against the tree tops, and I fly right over them, just brush them with my arms out. Over the whole town like an airplane. Spreading this salt frost in the autumn. I love autumn. And when the sun comes up—
ROBERT. Right.

EVA. It blinds you!

ROBERT. I've seen it.

EVA. It's so bright it blinds you. I want to fly like that, all over the town, right over everybody. It's beautiful. Listen. (*Skelly has taken one step forward.*) Did you hear something?

ROBERT. No. What?

EVA. Like something rustling in the leaves?

ROBERT. No. What? It was probably a rabbit. (*Skelly steps forward again, behind Nelly.*)

EVA. Listen.

ROBERT. I don't hear anything.

EVA. (*She and Robert cross D. R.*) Maybe it was the wind.

ROBERT. There isn't any; maybe it was a fox.

EVA. Don't.

ROBERT. (*Circles Cora.*) Or a wolf.

EVA. Ted Caffey trapped a wolf in his barn last year.

ROBERT. (*Crosses to post R.*) Shot its head off too.

EVA. Oh, he did not, are you trying to scare me; it got away.

ROBERT. Shot it and killed it; took its pelt in to the county agent in Centerville and got twenty dollars for it.

EVA. It wasn't anything; we better get back.

ROBERT. It was probably the mate looking for the one Caffey shot. (*Crosses to Eva C.*)

EVA. Don't say that, it wasn't— (*Skelly crosses behind Josh, R. on second platform.*) Listen!

ROBERT. It wasn't anything. (*Eva and Robert D. C. turn U. and lights up on "cafe."*)

WALTER. What's that junk heap of a what was it a Plymouth?

CORA. At Church Street? That's Driver's car. Driver Junior's older brother. Drove it in stock car races; over in Centerville they have a track. The whole town went; used to, when he drove. I suppose they think it's bad luck now, he had some kind of accident; smashed it to hell, it looks like, doesn't it?

WALTER. He get killed?

CORA. Oh, yes, killed instantly. They hitched up a chain to the car and pulled it back here.

WALTER. And dumped it in the middle of the street? The grass and weeds almost cover it; I didn't know what it was at first.

CORA. Well, that's where the chain broke and the axle broke and

56

every other damn thing broke, so there it sits. Not a very pretty sight. (*Lights out on "cafe" and an evening glow on stage, without "leaves" effect.—From "tree" positions characters move into similar positions and situations that lines are taken from. Each one in own world.*)

MARY. Rusting away—flaking away.

EVELYN. Falling apart, boarded together, everything flapping and rusting.

MARY. All the buildings bowing and nodding.

PATSY. Movie house been closed down eight years.

TRUCKER. Can't avoid it. I guess.

NELLY. You fall down, you bruise, you run into things, you're old.

WILMA. The wages of sin lead to death.

PATSY. Tumbleweed blowing down the deserted streets.

MARY. And the flowers dry up and die.

SKELLY. You didn't go to the race to see him kill himself.

PECK. —You watch yourself.

EVA. And it covers everything and that's rime. (*To help the actors and confine movement, each actor moves two lines ahead of his into position and one line after his back into "trees."*)

LENA. I remember his laugh.

CORA. Eldritch is all but a ghost town.

MARTHA. I don't know, love.

EVA. And when the sun comes up it blinds you!

EVELYN. The mine shaft building used to just shine.

SKELLY. All in the air.

JOSH. Just see.

LENA. It's a beautiful church.

WALTER. Wouldn't you say?

MAVIS. A decent person is afraid to move outside at night.

PREACHER. As you go your way tonight.

CORA. You seem uneasy.

EVELYN. The doctor said it was just shock.

MARY. Gone, gone gone.

EVA. Like it's been dipped in water then in sugar.

MAVIS. And not seen the light of day tomorrow.

MARY. All my children.

EVA. And that's what I want to be.

MARY. Gone, gone gone. (*Leaf effect up. Back into the "forest."*)

EVA. You know what my mother says?

ROBERT. What?

EVA. When I come in?

ROBERT. What?

EVA. She says you're unresponsible, and she asks me things like where we go and all, everywhere we go ever time I go anywhere with you. Everything we do.

ROBERT. Where does she think we go?

EVA. Oh, I tell her we just go walking in the woods; talking. She knows that but she thinks we do other things too.

ROBERT. Like what?

EVA. You know.

ROBERT. Like what?

EVA. You know. Dirty things. (*Turns away.*)

ROBERT. (*Crosses* D. R.) What does she think that for?

EVA. I don't tell her, though.

ROBERT. What would you tell her?

EVA. About that. About when I have to pee and things. (*Looks away from Robert.*)

ROBERT. Well, there's nothing dirty about that.

EVA. Well, don't you think I know! (*Crosses* U. C. *and sits on edge of top platform.*)

ROBERT. She means other things.

EVA. What?

ROBERT. Never mind.

EVA. Well don't you think I know? I know. You don't do things like that, you don't even look! I can though; I know.

ROBERT. You don't know anything.

EVA. I DO TOO! I've seen. You think I'm so young because I'm so little. I'm fourteen; I can have babies already; and I've seen cows do it when they're in heat. But you wouldn't do something like that.

ROBERT. Let's go back. (*Crosses* U. *second platform.*)

EVA. (*Stands.*) Let's do. I know how; I can.

ROBERT. When cows are in heat that's one cow jumping on another; you don't know anything.

EVA. You're ashamed; (*Robert crosses to post.*) you're not old enough to.

ROBERT. (*At post.*) You don't know what you're talking about.

EVA. Boys have to be older. But I'll bet your brother could anyway. I might as well because she thinks we do anyway. You're the one who doesn't know anything about it.

ROBERT. I should just to show you (*Eva starts hopping* D. C.) —don't—you don't know what you're talking about.

EVA. What?

ROBERT. Anything. Because you don't know anything about it.

EVA. I do too. You're afraid. (*Turns away.*)

ROBERT. You don't know what you're talking about even. (*Lines begin to overlap.*)

EVA. Only not here.

ROBERT. Why not? What's wrong with here?

EVA. You have to be in bed, stupid!

ROBERT. If you think you know so much. (*Grabbing her. Throwing her to ground.*)

EVA. (*Violently.*) Let go of me! You leave me alone. I will if I want to. (*Breaks away, circles Cora. Robert follows.*)

ROBERT. You want to get it in you so bad! You think I can't.

EVA. Stop it.

ROBERT. You think I won't do it. (*Throws her down again* D. C. *Lights up on top platform.*)

EVA. Leave me alone. I'll tell.

ROBERT. No you won't; you asked for it.

MARY. Nelly, Nelly, there's someone out back, honey, having a terrible fight; they came through the woods and started yelling all kinds of things.

NELLY. Where was you? I thought you was in bed.

MARY. You better go out and see, honey. (*Nelly crosses* U. L. C., *gets hidden shotgun.*)

ROBERT. (*Over.*) No you won't tell; you asked for it.

EVA. Leave me alone.

ROBERT. You think you're so smart; I'll show you. Shut up now, shut up or I'll kill you anyway; you asked for it. (*Eva saying "no, stay away," over and over. Struggling violently on the ground.*) You little whore; you think I won't, I'll show you. Stop it.

EVA. Leave me alone. Leave me alone. Don't touch me.

SKELLY. (*From the group, breaking toward them.*) What do you think—leave her alone. Don't hurt her. Robert. Don't hurt her.

59

(*He pulls Robert off Eva, Eva, still screaming, Robert thrown to the ground.*) Get up.

NELLY. (*At u. l. with the shotgun, throwing open the "door."*) What's going on? Who's there? (*Eva screams, half out of mortification, Skelly looks up and runs toward Nelly instinctively.*)

SKELLY. Help her! (*As Eva screams, Nelly levels the shotgun at Skelly's chest and fires first one then the other barrel at him. The Congregation moves from their stationary positions, mill a brief moment. The gun is passed, without much interest from one to the other of six people, Wilma, Martha, Josh, Peck, Mavis and Trucker. Skelly falls slowly to the ground. The Congregation assembles at the court, hiding Skelly. Patsy and Walter cross u. c. out of sight.*)

LENA. (*Immediately after the shots, as lights go slowly into "court room." Skelly is dead c. after gun is passed. Trucker, Peck, Josh stand d. of him looking u. c. at Judge who places gun on floor.*) It's a beautiful church.

JUDGE. State your name.

ROBERT. Robert Conklin.

JUDGE. Do you swear to tell the whole truth and nothing but the truth so help you God?

ROBERT. I do.

JUDGE. There's nothing to be nervous about, Robert. We want you to tell the court, just in your own words, what happened on the night in question. Can you do that?

ROBERT. Yes, I think.

JUDGE. We know this has been a terrible shock to you—

ROBERT. —I'm okay, I think. See—Eva and I were walking. We do quite frequently. Just wandering through the woods, talking. And we noticed that it had begun to get dark so we thought we had better start back—and we were heading back towards the main street, that would be West. And Eva thought she heard something behind us and we listened but we didn't hear it again so I assumed we were hearing things. Or it was our imagination. And it got dark pretty fast. And we were just coming into the clearing right behind the mill. Windrod's mill. And uh, we heard something again and this time we saw something behind the trees and we started running. More as a joke than anything—and then he started running too. And it was Skelly, and I wasn't afraid of him, but I knew he'd never liked my brother, and he started running too. He must have been following us all the time; everybody knows how he spies on people; I guess just as we broke into the clearing—and he came from nowhere. (*Crowd reaction.*) And he took us by surprise and he pushed me—he hit me from behind; I don't know if I passed out or not. (*Crowd murmur.*) He's immensely strong. (*Crowd murmur.*) And I heard a ringing in my ears and I saw what he was trying to do, and everything went white. And he pushed me.

EVA. (*Standing up. Hugely loud.*) AHHHHHHHHHHH! AHHHHHHHHHHHH! AHHHHHHHHHHHHH!

EVELYN. Oh, god, oh god, baby, my baby.

EVA. NO! no, no, no, no, no.

EVELYN. See her crippled body. See her broken back; why? Why has God cursed me with this burden? I don't complain, I ask why? We love Him. We bless Him. Praise Him. (*Everyone freezes. Tableau. Silence.*)

PATSY. (*Off. Everyone motionless as lights fade in slow, slow count.*) You know I saw you the day you first came into town, I'll bet. I've seen you a lot. Up at the Hilltop. I told Lena I liked you. No, no, come on. Yes, it's all right; I want you to. You know I do.

WALTER. (*Off.*) I've got nothing with me.

PATSY. (*Off.*) I know, it doesn't matter. You wouldn't wash your feet with your socks on. Be easy. Did you know, I'd watched you? Huh? Did you? Huh? Did you know I had?

WALTER. No. I've seen you a couple of times.

PATSY. I told Lena I liked you. I don't like any of the boys here; they're terrible, shiftless; oh, they're all right. But nobody wants to spend their life here; not here in this place rotting away. Walter! Your name's Walter, isn't it? I found out. (*Trucker crosses* R.) Oh. Oh, I love you, Walter. I do. I really do. I love you. (*Peck crosses* R.) Oh, I do. Really. Did you know that? I have since I saw you that first time. (*Josh crosses* R., *revealing Skelly.*) I do. I really do. I love you so much. I love you, oh, I do, I love you. I do. Oh, I love you, Walter. You're the only one I love; I do. Really, I do. (*Slow fade of light only on Skelly and then complete fade to black.*)

CURTAIN

(Hymn to be sung in Act I)

SHALL WE GATHER AT THE RIVER

Shall we gather at the river
Where bright angels' feet have trod
With its crystal tides forever
Flowing by the throne of God
Yes we'll gather at the river
The beautiful, the beautiful river
Gather with the saints at the river
That flows by the throne of God . . .

(Hymn to be sung in Act II)

WHEN THE TRUMPETS OF THE LORD SHALL SOUND

When the trumpets of the Lord shall sound
And time shall be no more
And the morning breaks eternal bright and fair—
When the saints of earth shall gather
Over on the other shore—
And the roll is called up yonder I'll be there—

When the roll is called up yonder

PROPERTY PLOT

On stage:

Double-barreled shotgun (hidden on platform)

NEW PLAYS

★ **THE CIDER HOUSE RULES, PARTS 1 & 2 by Peter Parnell, adapted from the novel by John Irving.** Spanning eight decades of American life, this adaptation from the Irving novel tells the story of Dr. Wilbur Larch, founder of the St. Cloud's, Maine orphanage and hospital, and of the complex father-son relationship he develops with the young orphan Homer Wells. "...luxurious digressions, confident pacing...an enterprise of scope and vigor..." *–NY Times*. "...The fact that I can't wait to see Part 2 only begins to suggest just how good it is..." *–NY Daily News*. "...engrossing...an odyssey that has only one major shortcoming: It comes to an end." *–Seattle Times*. "...outstanding...captures the humor, the humility...of Irving's 588-page novel..." *–Seattle Post-Intelligencer*. [9M, 10W, doubling, flexible casting] PART 1 ISBN: 0-8222-1725-2 PART 2 ISBN: 0-8222-1726-0

★ **TEN UNKNOWNS by Jon Robin Baitz.** An iconoclastic American painter in his seventies has his life turned upside down by an art dealer and his ex-boyfriend. "...breadth and complexity...a sweet and delicate harmony rises from the four cast members...Mr. Baitz is without peer among his contemporaries in creating dialogue that spontaneously conveys a character's social context and moral limitations..." *–NY Times*. "...darkly funny, brilliantly desperate comedy...TEN UNKNOWNS vibrates with vital voices." *–NY Post*. [3M, 1W] ISBN: 0-8222-1826-7

★ **BOOK OF DAYS by Lanford Wilson.** A small-town actress playing St. Joan struggles to expose a murder. "...[Wilson's] best work since *Fifth of July*...An intriguing, prismatic and thoroughly engrossing depiction of contemporary small-town life with a murder mystery at its core...a splendid evening of theater..." *–Variety*. "...fascinating...a densely populated, unpredictable little world." *–St. Louis Post-Dispatch*. [6M, 5W] ISBN: 0-8222-1767-8

★ **THE SYRINGA TREE by Pamela Gien.** Winner of the 2001 Obie Award. A breathtakingly beautiful tale of growing up white in apartheid South Africa. "Instantly engaging, exotic, complex, deeply shocking...a thoroughly persuasive transport to a time and a place...stun[s] with the power of a gut punch..." *–NY Times*. "Astonishing...affecting ...[with] a dramatic and heartbreaking conclusion...A deceptive sweet simplicity haunts THE SYRINGA TREE..." *–A.P.* [1W (or flexible cast)] ISBN: 0-8222-1792-9

★ **COYOTE ON A FENCE by Bruce Graham.** An emotionally riveting look at capital punishment. "The language is as precise as it is profane, provoking both troubling thought and the occasional cheerful laugh...will change you a little before it lets go of you." *–Cincinnati CityBeat*. "...excellent theater in every way..." *–Philadelphia City Paper*. [3M, 1W] ISBN: 0-8222-1738-4

★ **THE PLAY ABOUT THE BABY by Edward Albee.** Concerns a young couple who have just had a baby and the strange turn of events that transpire when they are visited by an older man and woman. "An invaluable self-portrait of sorts from one of the few genuinely great living American dramatists...rockets into that special corner of theater heaven where words shoot off like fireworks into dazzling patterns and hues." *–NY Times*. "An exhilarating, wicked...emotional terrorism." *–NY Newsday*. [2M, 2W] ISBN: 0-8222-1814-3

★ **FORCE CONTINUUM by Kia Corthron.** Tensions among black and white police officers and the neighborhoods they serve form the backdrop of this discomfiting look at life in the inner city. "The creator of this intense...new play is a singular voice among American playwrights...exceptionally eloquent..." *–NY Times*. "...a rich subject and a wise attitude." *–NY Post*. [6M, 2W, 1 boy] ISBN: 0-8222-1817-8

DRAMATISTS PLAY SERVICE, INC.
440 Park Avenue South, New York, NY 10016 212-683-8960 Fax 212-213-1539
postmaster@dramatists.com www.dramatists.com